HUNTING BIN LADEN

HUNTING BIN LADEN

HOW AL-QAEDA IS WINNING
THE WAR ON TERROR

Rob Schultheis

SKYHORSE PUBLISHING

Skyhorse Publishing books may be purchased in bulk at special discounts for sales promotion, corporate gifts, fund raising, or educational purposes. Special editions can also be created to specifications. For details, contact Special Sales Department, Skyhorse Publishing, 555 Eighth Avenue, Suite 903, New York, NY 10018 or info@skyhorsepublishing.com.

www.skyhorsepublishing.com

Library of Congress Cataloging-in-Publication Data

Schultheis, Rob.
    Hunting Bin Laden : how Al-Qaeda is winning the war on terror / Rob Schultheis.
        p. cm.
    Includes bibliographical references and index.
    ISBN 978-1-60239-244-1 (alk. paper)
    1. Qaida (Organization) 2. Terrorism. 3. Bin Laden, Osama, 1957- I. Title.

HV6432.5.Q2S36 2008
909.83'1—dc22   2008010552

10 9 8 7 6 5 4 3 2 1

Printed in the United States of America

In memory of Professor Syed Burhauddin Majrooh,
Sergeant Robert Paul, U.S. Army (Reserve), and all the other
people around the world martyred by the global
Wahhabi/Salafi conspiracy.

To "Mycroft," without whose help this book
could not have been written.

CONTENTS

CHAPTER 1

9/11: THE EARTHQUAKE
THAT NEVER WAS

On September 9, 2001, a group of sixty-nine Saudi Arabians arrived in Las Vegas from the L.A. area and checked into suites at the Four Seasons and Caesar's Palace. To quote from the FBI field report on the matter, "It is understood that the group traveled from the Los Angeles area via chartered aircraft and rented automobiles. *The group departed the Los Angeles area in response to their fears about further earthquakes following a tremor in the Los Angeles area on or about 09/08/2001*." Throughout the FBI report, the group is referred to as "*the Saudi Arabian royal party and their entourage* [italics in both sentences mine]."

When the news on the 9/11 attacks came in two days later, the Saudis at Caesar's Palace checked out and joined their friends at the Four Seasons, where the group occupied fifty-six rooms. By the end of the day the entire group was being protected by a large contingent of armed personnel from the elite Beverly Hills security company

FAM. Despite this, one of them told an unidentified FBI agent that
the "Saudi Arabian royalty were extremely concerned about their
personal safety, and the safety of their mostly Middle Eastern entourage, in the wake of the Twin Towers/Pentagon//PA [Pennsylvania]
attacks." The Saudis told the Las Vegas agents that they wanted to
charter a flight out of the U.S. as soon as possible.

For the next week the Saudi group repeatedly tried to book a
charter flight out of the United States, but with no luck, according to
the FBI report. Finally, on September 18, they succeeded. Whether
the FBI assisted them by playing travel agent isn't clear; the many
blank spaces in the report, made for "security reasons," leave that
question unanswered. The document does state that on the eigh-
teenth two agents met with a representative of the Saudi group to
review passenger manifests and passports, and on the nineteenth,
fifty-one of the Saudis boarded a Republic of Gabon–registered
DC-8 bound for London; FBI agents helped provide security at the
boarding area. The next day, the remaining eighteen Saudis flew out
of Las Vegas for London on a chartered 727-21, with the FBI again
safeguarding their departure.

As we all know now, sixteen of the nineteen hijackers who
attacked the United States on September 11, 2001, were citizens of
Saudi Arabia, and all were members of al-Qaeda, a multinational
Islamist group headed by another Saudi, Osama bin Laden.
Al-Qaeda is funded by some of the richest, most powerful people in
Saudi Arabia, including members of the royal family.

The Southern California Saudi community had close ties to at least two of the 9/11 hijackers, Nawaf al-Hazmi and Khalid Almihdhar. When the two young Saudi Arabians arrived at LAX from Southeast Asia early in 2000, they spoke almost no English and reportedly had little money; the day they landed, they were taken in by Omar al-Bayoumi, a Saudi who was a long-time resident of San Diego and who owned an apartment building there. When he was questioned after 9/11, al-Bayoumi told investigators he had never met the two men before; he happened to be at the airport in Los Angeles that day, overheard them talking in Arabic, and decided on the spot to help them. After giving them $1,500 in cash, he let them move into his apartment building, got them Social Security cards, and helped them apply for flight school.

Over the next several months, al-Bayoumi and two of his associates reportedly received a series of checks worth from $3,500 to $15,000 from Prince Bandar bin Sultan and his wife Princess Haifa, daughter of the late Saudi King Faisal. Prince Bandar is an old friend of many American presidents, vice presidents and congressmen, and for many years was the Saudi ambassador to the United States. Bandar and his wife claim that they thought the funds were going to charitable institutions aiding innocent Saudi immigrants in the U.S. Al-Bayoumi passed the money on to al-Hazmi and Almihdhar, allowing them to live quietly in the U.S. until, on September 11, 2001, they and three other men hijacked an American Airlines 757 and crashed it into the Pentagon.

Some months after 9/11, al-Bayoumi was picked up by British authorities in London and questioned about his role in relaying money to the hijacker and his connections with Saudi officials in that regard. He denied everything, even when investigators found the private phone numbers of Saudi diplomats in papers concealed beneath the floorboards of his London apartment. Inexplicably, he was then released, immediately flew home to the safety of Saudi Arabia, and hasn't been seen since.

For her part, Princess Haifa claimed she thought the checks she wrote were going to a legitimate Saudi charity, and had no idea they had been used to fund terrorist attacks against the United States.

Evidence regarding this and other financial links between leading Saudi Arabians and al-Qaeda was blacked out in the 9/11 Commission Report on the attacks, and all attempts to pursue the issue later have been systematically stonewalled at the highest levels of our government. "Follow the money" is the recognized key to unraveling any conspiracy; by covering up the financing behind the 9/11 plot, the very U.S. officials sworn to protect this country and its citizens have ensured that the people behind the worst terrorist attack in history, an attack that killed over three thousand Americans, have so far gone unpunished.

And that earthquake that supposedly triggered the mass exodus of Saudi royalty from Los Angeles two days before 9/11? Records from the Southern California Earthquake Center show that it was a relatively minor tremor, 4.1 on the Richter scale, so small that it didn't make the evening news on network television; it caused no injuries, and the only property damage resulted from objects falling off tables, shelves, and mantelpieces, and no one in the seismological community predicted that it might be the precursor of another, larger quake.

Whatever drove the Saudi royal party to flee from L.A. two days before the terrorist attacks on the United States, it seems very, very unlikely it was the nonexistent threat of a major earthquake.

· · ·

There's never been a stranger war than the one America has been waging since the events on 9/11. Today, a half decade later, we are occupying Iraq, which had nothing to do with the attacks; are trying to destabilize Iran, which had nothing to do with the attacks; and are threatening Syria, which had nothing to do with the attacks, with forcible regime change. Meanwhile Saudi Arabia and Pakistan, the real powers behind 9/11, continue to receive tens of billions of dollars in U.S. aid, and are totally unmolested.

One army officer I knew in Iraq put it this way: "It's as if on December 8, 1941, we declared war on Brazil, Iceland, and New Zealand, and announced that Japan, Germany, and Italy were our closest allies in the conflict."

I will have much more to say about the role of Pakistan's military intelligence apparat, ISI, in 9/11 and other more current anti-American activities, but I'll bring up just one glaring piece of circumstantial evidence here. When I was in Taleban-controlled Afghanistan, ISI and al-Qaeda's Arabs were omnipresent; every government office in Kabul had its ISI officers in mufti and Arabs lurking in the background, calling the shots. The ISI knew *everything* that went on inside Afghanistan; even back when the Soviets occupied the country, their eyes and ears were everywhere. I remember coming back from a long walk/horseback ride through the combat zones in eastern Afghanistan back then, and being called in to the local ISI office in Peshawar immediately upon my return. I had warm relations with ISI back then, partially because we shared common friends in the global intel community. After all, we were more or less on the same side.

Over cups of tea, the officers there showed me on the map everywhere I had been on my trip, told me everyone I had met and talked to in chaishops, villages, and *marcazs* (guerrilla bases), and what we had talked about. And this was while Afghanistan was occupied by the Soviet Union, when journalists and ISI agents alike had to do their work on the run, invisibly!

This all clicked when I saw a videotape released by al-Qaeda on September 11, 2006, to celebrate the anniversary of the attacks. In the tape, Osama bin Laden is shown talking with head hijacker Mohammed Atta about the plot; the two are sitting out in the open in one of the training camps in Afghanistan, within earshot of countless other people. It is 100 percent impossible to believe that someone in ISI, or an ISI informant, didn't know about the plot; and

A few lucky guerrilla bands had acquired 12.7 and 14.5 millimeter heavy machine guns and recoilless rifles, and occasionally a camel or train of pack horses managed to bring in a few thousand black market Italian antitank mines, but for the most part the Afghan resistance ran on pure grit, the faith and fervor of jihad, holy war.

My interpreter friend Sher Mohammed and I had entered Afghanistan from Pakistan with a *mujahedin* caravan delivering supplies to the front lines southeast of Kabul. The commander of the group we were with, Anwar, had a base in the bombed-out village of Jegdeleg, from which he mounted attacks on the Kabul-Jalalabad highway and the hydroelectric power plant at Soroobi. It took us two days to get there from the border, a rugged journey across the Safed Koh, the White Mountains, through one bombed-out, abandoned village after another, past the flag-decked graves of *shaheed*, martyrs, most of them civilian refugees killed while fleeing the fighting.

The skies were alive with enemy aircraft, cruising imperiously, virtually omnipotent; we were never out of sight of one, two, or more of them. Here a quartet of deadly Mi-24 helicopter gunships loitered, looking for kills; each chopper packed dozens of air to surface rockets and a rotary nose cannon that fired six hundred rounds per minute, and they often carried one or two thousand-pound bombs. A few miles to the south another pair of gunships crossed a ridge and descended into the next valley. There was a high ripple of thunder, a sound something like a giant block of iron being dragged across a marble floor, and craning our necks we saw two MiGs bisecting the

CHAPTER 2

BEFORE THERE WAS AL-QAEDA, THERE WAS AL-QAEDA

I first met al-Qaeda before there was an al-Qaeda, way back in the winter of 1984; it was an encounter that came within a split second of costing me my life.

It was my second trip into wartime Afghanistan, a hard time for the anti-Soviet *mujahedin*. After five years of fighting, the Red Army's superior firepower and willingness to use it on civilians and guerrillas alike was beginning to take its toll on the resistance. The *muj* were brave, and stubborn as only Afghans can be, but they were outgunned to a surreal degree: they faced an armada of helicopter gunships and jets, thousands of tanks and armored personnel carriers, heavy artillery and truck-mounted multi-tube rocket launchers; their ragtag arsenal consisted of ancient Enfield carbines, homemade booby traps, and a smattering of AK-47 assault rifles and bazooka-like RPG-7s.

only slightly less likely that they, and the wealthy Saudis who funded the attacks, weren't active participants, from start to finish. There is much, much more hard evidence, to be discussed later.

The truth of the matter is, the real Axis of Evil is ISI, leading members of the Saudi Arabian ruling class, and the violent extremist Sunni groups, like Taleban, al-Qaeda, and the Moslem Brotherhood, that Saudi Arabia funds and sponsors around the globe. And while we tilt at windmills, this unholy troika remains in the shadows, growing stronger, smarter, bigger, and more elusive, its goal nothing less than taking over the entire Islamic world, and after that, the rest of us. And as we are perceived as being in the way, we have to be totally destroyed for the goal to be achieved.

sky with parallel contrails. To the north, where we were headed, an Antonov turboprop cut lazy circles in the sky, back and forth: it was a spy plane equipped with cameras, the Afghans said, that could take your portrait from ten thousand feet up and zap it to Kabul in an instant. It all made you feel incredibly vulnerable, as if all your nerve endings were poking out through your naked skin; a world of hurt, without safety, shelter, rules.

The last few hours of the trek we passed through an area of barren badlands, where the only cover was provided by sparse shoulder-high trees. The countryside around the trail was littered with anti-personnel mines, small butterfly-shaped plastic devices scattered from the air, their tan color designed to blend in with the ground; they were designed to maim instead of kill, the idea being that a man with his foot or leg blown off was a greater psychological blow to an insurgency than a dead one, especially since the Afghans believed that anyone killed in a jihad went straight to Paradise.

The *mujahedin* called this stretch the Trail of Death, for the scores of travelers, guerrillas, and civilians caught here and killed by enemy aircraft, and we had a narrow escape ourselves that day, crossing that sinister zone. The caravan was winding down a *nullah*, a dry river bed, when a roar like a minotaur's cry came rolling down the gorge from our rear. The lead packhorses were just entering a deep narrow cleft in the rock, the only cover for miles in either direction; the *muj* drove the animals into a gallop, and they vanished into the shadowy depths of the canyon just as two MiGs came into view, following the trail less than a hundred feet up. I had been lagging behind, and as the two jets passed, wingtip to wingtip, the pilots angled down to take a good look at me. I was dressed like an Afghan, in a loose *shalwar kameez*, long shirt and baggy trousers, and all they saw was a lone native, a peasant or peddler, perhaps a Sufi pilgrim, trudging through the dust and stones; the caravan was safely out of sight, hidden by cliff and shadow. For an interminable split second the two pilots and I locked eyes, and then the two deadly jets swerved and were gone, rocketing on down the ravine. The sound of their engines faded away in the air and disappeared into silence, I rejoined my companions a few moments later, in the shelter of the slot canyon; they hugged me, and we all began to laugh, the unequivocal laughter of lucky survivors.

When we arrived at Anwar's *marcaz* (base) in Jegdeleg at dusk, Sher Mohammed and I were greeted warmly by the small band of fighters there. Foreigners rarely visited the *mujahedin* back then, and anyone who did, journalist, aid worker, doctor, whatever, was regarded as a kind of honorary supporter of the jihad. Only one person stood apart, a young man, handsome in an effete way, with a neatly-trimmed spade-shaped beard, clad in spotless white robes. When I smiled at him he glared back at me, his eyes radiating an almost palpable hostility. Sher Mohammed questioned the *mujahedin* and learned that the man was a Saudi Arabian from a wealthy family in Riyadh; he had heard about the Afghans' battle against the infidel Russians, and had decided to come over to try and help them. He had brought several thousand dollars in cash, to contribute to the jihad, and he told the Afghans he was going to raise more money for them when he went home to Riyadh.

That night in the cave-like room where the *muj* slept the Saudi youth led the Afghans in prayer. He recited the creed in a loud theatrical voice; whenever he mentioned God, he sang out *"A-llah"* with lip-smacking fervor. A couple of times I noticed some of the young Afghan fighters exchange glances: evidently they found their coreligionist benefactor a bit of a queer duck. The Afghans liked to do their praying quietly, each man muttering his prayers under his breath, for God's ears alone. When everyone turned in later that night—we all slept on thin mattresses on the floor—the Saudi was still giving me the evil eye.

I rose early the next morning, wakened by the *mujahedin* doing their dawn prayers, and the Saudi was gone. I asked Sher Mohammed where he had was, and he replied vaguely that he had "gone away," either back to Pakistan or to another *marcaz* in the area . . .

It wasn't until we returned to Pakistan that Sher Mohammed told me what had happened during that night at Jegdeleg. He hadn't trusted the Saudi Arabian, so he had lain awake, pretending to sleep, one eye on the young Arab. Sometime in the middle of the night, the Saudi rose silently and crept between the slumbering Afghans to where the weapons were stacked by the door. He took an AK-47, made sure it was loaded, and then he tiptoed stealthily toward where I was sleeping. As he raised the gun to fire, Sher Mohammed leapt on him, ripped the AK from his hands, and dragged him out the door.

I must have been totally exhausted after two days on the trail, because I slept through it all, but the *mujahedin* in the room woke in time to see what had happened. They were furious, Sher Mohammed told me; I was a guest in their village, with their tribe, and my death while I was there would have cast an indelible stain on their honor. After a fierce whispered conference they marched the would-be assassin out to the edge of the ruined village and hurled him out onto the trail. Sher Mohammed watched him limp out of sight, a wretched figure in a torn white robe, bruised, bleeding, heading south toward the Pakistan border. A year or two later a horde of others like him would be in Afghanistan; one of them would be Osama bin Laden.

•   •   •

Foreigners who didn't understand Afghanistan described it as a land of religious fanatics, bloodthirsty holy warriors who hated all non-Moslems, but I had found the reality to be radically different. Afghan society was still tribal, and people still lived according to an ancient code of honor, one of whose linchpins was *melmestia*, hospitality to strangers. "*Musafir aziz khoda,*" went the Afghan saying: "The traveler is beloved by God."

The Pushtuns, the dominant tribal group in the country, liked to tell the story of a chieftain in the mountains whose only and much-loved son was murdered by a member of a rival clan. One day the murderer found himself being pursued by warriors from a clan allied with the chieftain's; he ended up in the chieftain's village, and came to the open gate of the chief's compound. Not knowing what else to do, where else to go, he entered the compound, threw himself at the chieftain's feet, and placed himself under the his protection. According to the tribal code called *pushtunwali* the chieftain had the right to kill his son's murderer on the spot; the doctrine of *badal*, blood feud, decreed an eye for an eye, a death for a death, when one's relative or fellow clan or tribe member was killed by an outsider. But *melmestia* trumped vengeance. When the mob of pursuers reached the compound, they found the chieftain standing in the entrance, sword in his hand, his son's murderer behind him. "If you want to kill him, you must first kill me," the chieftain said. "No matter what he has done in the past, he is under my protection now." The tale ends with the chief dying to protect the man he hates more than anyone on earth. Honor, fearlessness, generosity of spirit: the story embodied all of the Afghans' most treasured values.

The Afghans' religious beliefs complemented their tribal traditions perfectly. Ninety percent of all Afghans were followers of the moderate Hanafi school of Sunni Islam, permeated with Sufism, the mystical form of Islam that stresses personal experience of the divine and rejects orthodoxy and dogma. Every Afghan, even illiterate farmers, truck drivers, and peddlers, could quote from memory the words of Afghanistan's famous Sufi poet Hakim Sanai: "At God's door, what's the difference between Moslem and Christian, virtuous and guilty?"

If you came to their country peacefully, with a modicum of respect for their beliefs and customs, they were the very soul of tolerance. They·loved to debate religion with Christians, Jews, and other non-Moslems; nothing delighted them more than an endless palaver about prophets, angels, djinns, and right and wrong, fuelled by countless cups of *toor chai* (black tea) and *sheen chai* (green tea), and if they didn't manage to convert you into a good Moslem in the end (their poorly disguised hope) they didn't seem to really mind.

One incident on my first trip into the war zone particularly lodged in my mind. Sher Mohammed and I along with two or three guerrillas were on our way from Pakistan to Dobanday, a *mujahedin* center hidden in a deep gorge southeast of Kabul, and at one point we stopped to rest in the rubble of a bombed-out village in the badland foothills of the Safed Koh. The place had been utterly destroyed: every building was gone, including the community mosque, blasted into lumps of adobe, splintered timbers and dust; the abandoned fields had dried up, and the orchards were dying or dead. All the inhabitants were gone, fled to the crowded refugee camps in Pakistan; only a dozen or so youths remained, camping out in the ruins, subsisting on bread and tea and fighting the Russians with old Enfield carbines and a couple of secondhand Kalashnikovs. They were a wild bunch, angry-eyed, sinewy, and sunburnt, in dust-colored clothes. They smoked hashish constantly in their buurow-like *marcaz*, till the air was cloying, thick with dreams.

That evening, they gathered in the empty plaza amid the ruins to pray toward Mecca; when they saw I wasn't joining them, they gathered around Sher Mohammed, gesturing toward me and asking him what was wrong. I had never been with the *muj* before, and I looked on nervously, imagining an Islamic version of the Inquisition: "Who is this infidel, and why doesn't he pray to God the way we and all good people do?"

Instead, they came over to me with a smiling Sher Mohammed in tow. "They want to know if you have a pencil and paper," he said, as the *muj* looked on expectantly.

"Why?" I asked.

"I told them that you were a Christian, and that Christians always pray in a building called a 'church.' They want you to draw them a picture of one, so they can build it before you return. They are ashamed that there is no place for you to pray in their village."

So much for the "intolerant Afghans" and their "fanatical religion."

• • •

Look at the overall history of Islam, and a couple of things instantly become clear: we need to stop referring to the struggle we currently find ourselves involved in as "the War on Terror," and we need to stop thinking it is between the United States and something called "Islamo-fascism."

The attacks on 9/11 were really a sideshow in the civil war that is currently raging within Islam, an internecine struggle whose roots stretch back to the very earliest years of the faith. On one side are the majority of Moslems whose focus is the future; who are slowly, painfully adapting their beliefs to the modern world; on the other, a fanatical minority who reject both future and present, and who look to the past, a past that never was, for salvation. Most of the innocent victims in this conflict have been moderate Moslems: in Afghanistan, the Taleban and al-Qaeda killed as many as 200,000 Shi'a members of the Hazara tribe, and allied groups in Pakistan have murdered hundreds of Shi'as, Alawites, and other Moslem minority groups over the last few decades. Until we join forces with progressive, pragmatic Moslems around the globe, we and they will be vulnerable to the kinds of asymmetrical warfare typified by 9/11, the assassinations of Anwar Sadat and Benazir Bhutto, and the suicide bombings that are now destabilizing Afghanistan, Pakistan, and Iraq.

Islam was founded in seventh-century Arabia, at a time of religious and political discord in the region. The Arabian Peninsula was populated by feuding tribes; some were converts to Christianity or Judaism, while others practiced the ancient polytheistic paganism of their ancestors. The center of Arabian paganism was Mecca, and it was there, in AD 610, that a forty-year-old merchant named Mohammed, disgusted with the city's corruption and decadence, retreated to a cave on a nearby mountainside in search of spiritual comfort. The series of visions he experienced, recorded in the Koran, became the basis of a new faith, one very much in the monotheistic tradition of Judaism and Christianity—Mohammed regarded himself as the successor to the great prophets of the Old and New Testaments—but uniquely Arab in character. The new religion was called Islam, meaning "submission," as in submission to God's teachings as revealed to Mohammed.

At first Mohammed's teachings gained few converts, most of them members of his family, slaves, and the poor and dispossessed. The pagan majority in Mecca, including Mohammed's own tribe, the Quraysh, had become wealthy catering to the pilgrims flocking to worship the idols in the city's central shrine, the Ka'aba; they resented the new prophet's uncompromising monotheism and anti-paganism on both religious and economic grounds.

In 622 the persecution of Mohammed and his followers became so harsh that the tiny Moslem community was forced to flee to the neighboring town of Medina. For the next eight years the Prophet's preaching gained more and more converts, and in 630 he returned to Mecca at the head of an army of ten thousand men and overthrew the city's pagan rulers; on his orders the idols were removed from the Ka'aba and destroyed, and the now-empty shrine became the central holy place of Islam. Mecca was only the beginning; when Mohammed died of a fever two years later, Islam had already spread across most of the Arabian Peninsula, and was rapidly making inroads in the surrounding regions.

What made Islam such an instant success story? After all, the metaphysical and ethical bedrock of Islam was unmistakably Judeo-Christian—there is one God, and His laws are laid down in the Ten Commandments—and Judaism and Christianity were already well established among the tribes of Arabia. What set Islam apart from these two older creeds, what was totally unique and original about Islam, was its strict code of behavior, which pervaded every aspect of everyday life, and which fit the austere traditional Arab mindset perfectly.

Anyone who converts to Islam agrees to the so-called Five Pillars. First, one accepts the creed called the *shahadat*: there is one true God, not many, that God is named "Allah," and Mohammed is Allah's messenger on earth (in Arabic, "*Allah illaha illa la, wa Mohammedan rasullah*"). Second, one must pray toward Mecca five times a day, at dawn, noon, late afternoon, sunset, and night; ideally, Moslems should also gather once a week, on Friday, and pray as a group. Third, Moslems must practice charity, or *zakat*, by donating at least one-fortieth of their income and wealth to the poor each year. (In reality, pious Moslems are usually far more generous. In 1972, when I was in Herat, in eastern Afghanistan, spring blizzards and floods had decimated the flocks and ravaged the tent encampments of the Kochi nomads in the area. The city's merchants not only fed, clothed, and housed the victims, they contributed enough money for them to buy new breeding stock and begin to replace their lost sheep and goats.)

The fourth pillar is the most rigorous: all Moslems must observe an annual month-long fast known as Ramadan, during which they neither eat nor drink from sunrise to sundown. Ramadan commemorates the hardships of Mohammed and his early followers when they were forced to flee from Mecca to Medina in 622.

Fifth and last, every Moslem, no matter where in the world they live, should attempt to make the Hajj, the pilgrimage to the holy city of Mecca, at least once in their life. During the peak of the yearly Hajj season, millions of the faithful gather from the ends of the earth, from every imaginable background: Afghan nomads, Turkish peasants, black African businessmen, blond blue-eyed Bosnian doctors, Indonesian fishermen. In aerial photographs taken at the height of the Hajj, hundreds of thousands of pilgrims, clad in white cotton robes, swirl around the shrine like iron filings gathered in by a powerful magnet.

All of this made Islam very different from Christianity, Judaism, paganism, and all of the world's other great religions, for that matter. With this code of behavior, Mohammed created not only a spiritual creed but a new kind of society, a kind of super-tribe, a borderless nation that was open to anyone on earth who accepted its strict tenets, regardless of ethnicity or cultural background. And it was a democratic society; according to Moslem tradition, the different races of mankind were created equal:

> The angel Izrail gathered dust from all parts of the earth—white, black and red dirt, soft and hard, which is why the complexions of the children of Adam are so varied, and why the Prophet said all the sons of Adam are the same, like teeth in a comb . . .

Once converted, a Moslem finds every aspect of his or her life has changed. The Five Pillars, along with the teachings of the Koran and the Hadith (the body of sayings traditionally attributed to the Prophet) and the code of *sharia* or theology-based law that has evolved over the centuries, rule every aspect of a devout believer's life.

Time is Moslem Time, from the prayers that rule each day, the weekly gathering at the mosque, and the yearly ordeal of Ramadan, to the Hajj that every Moslem hopes to carry out at least once in his or her life. And Space is sanctified as well, with Mecca at the center of the universe and the target for the prayers of all Moslems everywhere.

Even the language one thinks in changes: all Moslems everywhere, regardless of their native tongue, pray in the common liturgical language of Arabic that the Koran was written in. The beauty part of classical Arabic is its emotive power, even to someone who doesn't understand its meaning: anyone who has heard the *suras* (verses) of the Koran recited aloud, the rolling incantatory cadences, the strangely stirring strings of syllables, knows what a peculiarly potent vehicle spoken Arabic is in carrying a message, any message.

Islam began to split apart almost as soon as Mohammed died, with the dispute over who would succeed him as leader of the faith. And the tribe-like nature of the *ummah*, the global community of Moslem believers, guaranteed that the dispute would be bitter and uncompromising.

One side was led by Mohammed's wife Aisha, whose faction supported one of the Prophet's most prominent disciples, Abu Bakr; the other supported Ali, Mohammed's cousin, husband of the Prophet's daughter Fatima, and the second person to convert to Islam when Mohammed first began to reveal his divine message. Ali's followers called themselves the Shariat Ali, "Ali's followers," later shortened to "Shi'a"; Abu Bakr's faction became known as "Sunnis," from "sunnah," or "tradition," meaning the way of life of Mohammed, Abu Bakr, and the other original founders of Islam. This focus on the past as the source of salvation eventually led to the extreme fundamentalist groups causing so much trouble inside Islam and in the rest of the world today.

Over the next two decades, as Islam spread across the Arabian Peninsula into present-day Iraq, Iran, Syria, Palestine, North Africa, Armenia, and Turkey, the two factions fought a bloody civil war over who would be *caliph*, as the head of the faith came to be called. Abu Bakr, the first caliph, was poisoned, and his successor, Umar, was stabbed to death, both victims of feuds among their followers; the third caliph, Uthman, a Sunni like his two predecessors, died in battle. The Shi'a faction fared no better: Ali finally took power as the fourth caliph, but he was eventually murdered by one of his followers who thought he was too conciliatory toward the Sunnis.

The fate of Ali's two sons, Hassan and Hussein, further hardened the split in Islam. When Hassan told his followers not to fight against the Sunnis in order to preserve Islam's unity, they turned against him; a group of the most bitterly disaffected stabbed and badly wounded him. He retired from public life, continuing to stay aloof from the

Shi'a-Sunni power struggle while refusing the Sunnis' demands
that he join them in attacking another minority Islamic sect, the
Kharijites. Though his death a few years later was officially blamed
on natural causes, many Shi'ites believe he was poisoned to death on
orders from the Sunni leader Muawiyah, who wanted his son Yazd
to succeed Ali as the fifth caliph.

In AD 680, the Sunni-Shi'a conflict came to a climax, when Yazd
and an army of forty thousand men cornered Hussein, Hassan's
younger brother and Shi'a claimant to the position of caliph, near
the town of Karbala, in present-day Iraq. Hussein was accompanied
by less than a hundred supporters, almost all members of his family, including women, children, and old people; thousands of other
Moslems supported his cause, but when Hussein begged them to
come to his aid they declined to act. On the morning of October
10, after a day of furious fighting in which, according to legend,
Hussein personally killed more than four hundred foes, he and his
companions were slaughtered, even the elderly and the newborn
babies. From that day on, the Sunnis have been the dominant group
in Islam, while the Shi'as mourn the greatest tragedy ever to befall
mankind.

As Islam spread over a wider and wider territory, the Sunni caliphs
became more and more involved in earthly affairs like governance,
administration, and taxation. Much of what they did was positive:
they built housing for travelers and medical centers, increased charitable institutions for the poor, wrote tolerant laws guaranteeing the

rights of Jewish communities, and encouraged the arts and sciences. But inevitably there was negative side: as the state religion of what was essentially an empire, Sunni Islam lost much of its spiritual purity: the faith's leaders became rich and the rich got richer, and with wealth and inequality came corruption, bribery, and all the ugly, inevitable by-products of imperialism.

Over time, a pattern developed: whenever Sunnism was threatened from within by corruption or theological innovation or without from secularism or foreign imperialism, a certain number of Sunnis reacted by returning to the faith's roots in sunnah, tradition; to the past. Followers of this throwback theology call themselves Salafis, meaning "pious ancestors," referring to the supposed purity and spiritual perfection of the earliest Moslems. There are several different strands of Salafism today; al-Qaeda represents only one, and all of them possess that group's potential for catastrophic violence.

If modern Salafi movements have a common theological rootstock, it is the teachings of the thirteenth-century Syrian, Ahmad Ibnal-Taymiyyah. Al-Taymiyyah came along at a time when Islam was under siege by the Crusaders and the Mongols, and the current Islamic establishment seemingly lacked the vigor to defend itself.

Al-Taymiyya contrasted this sorry situation with the early glory-years of the faith, when the Prophet's followers swept irresistibly across the Arabian Peninsula and beyond, propelled by force of arms and the power of its message: despite Western portrayals of early Moslems spreading their faith solely by the sword, it was really the popularity of Mohammed's message and its ability to enlist converts from widely differing backgrounds into a rock-solid militant community that took it so far so fast.

Al-Taymiyya's message was fundamentally simple: if Moslems only returned to those glorious days of yesteryear, by re-creating the Islam of the Prophet and his companions, they would once again be successful. So went al-Taymiyya's thinking, and he mercilessly attacked anyone who dared disagree with him: this included Sufi mystics, with their emphasis on personal experience of the divine and saints who served as intermediaries with the divine; they were extremely popular at the time. All of the theologians, saints, and wise men who over the years had discovered new ways of expressing or interpreting Mohammed's teachings were guilty of apostasy: the only authentic guide to righteous behavior was contained in the lives of the Prophet and his immediate predecessors, and anyone who said or wrote anything else was no better than a *kfir*, an idolworshipper. Al-Taymiyya went even further: anyone who prayed to God for protection or strove to communicate with God diminished God's stature.

Perhaps unsurprisingly, al-Taymiyya spent much of his life in jail, under threat of execution, or apologizing for and disavowing his most outspoken ideas and abusive *ad hominem* attacks on rival theologians; but his ideas, as dour and sour as they were, lived on.

In nineteenth century Arabia, a rural theologian named Mohammed Ibn al-Wahhab, an admirer of al-Taymiyya's austere creed, saw an opportunity to empower it on earth by finding it a secular political ally. At that time, the relatively cosmopolitan Ottoman Turks ruled much of the Arab world; the Ottomans' sprawling territories were home to a wide variety of forms of Islam, everything from moderate schools of Sunnism to Sufism and other liberal forms of Islam.

The savvy al-Wahhab allied himself and his followers with the politically ambitious al-Saud tribe, who wanted to used the unifying power of ultraconservative Islam and anti-Turkish fervor to unite most of the Arabian Peninsula. The Ottomans succeeded in temporarily crushing the al-Sauds and their tribal allies, but in the mid-1920s a new al-Saud chief, twenty-year-old Abd al-Aziz, linked up with the Bedouin descendants of al-Wahhab's disciples, the Ikhwan or "Moslem Brotherhood," and succeeded in finally liberating the Arabian Peninsula once and for all. In 1932 the victorious al-Sauds formally established the nation of Saudi Arabia, and promptly suppressed the Ikhwan, who were a bit too politically active for their tastes; at the same time they made Wahhabism, a state-sponsored and controlled version of al-Wahhab's reactionary Sunnism, the nation's official religion. Thus was set the pattern that prevails in Saudi Arabia to this day: a monarchical regime, worldly and corrupt, that gives lip service to the extreme puritanical Sunni fundamentalism that helps keep it in power. The problem for the rest of the world is, the Saudi government spends hundreds of millions of dollars building Wahhabi mosques and madrassas around the world, spreading a militant, politically active, and often violent version of the faith that would never be allowed in Saudi Arabia itself. There are two basic reasons for this: some members of the vast Saudi royal family use the Wahhabi missionary movement to relieve fundamentalist pressure within Saudi Arabia and preserve their power base; others, genuine converts to Wahhabism's fanatical creed, look beyond the borders of Saudi Arabia, dreaming of an Islam and a world dominated by a Saudi-led Wahhabi theocracy.

Saudi Arabia is not the only country where Salafism has reappeared in the last century or two, almost always in response to a decline in Islam's fortunes. In the mid-nineteenth century, a group of Moslem scholars gathered in a small town north of Delhi and founded a madrassa called Dar-ul-Uloom, to promulgate a revitalized, politically active form of Islam. This resurgent brand of the faith was called Deobandism, after Deoband, the town's name. For centuries, the subcontinent's political power and culture had been based in the north, dominated by successive waves of Moslem invaders from Afghanistan and Central Asia. Now that the British had more or less unified India, Moslems found themselves a relatively weak minority group in a Hindu-dominated society. With a layer of British colonial overlords above that, the Deobandis looked back to their grand past and beyond, to the glory days of the Prophet and his disciples.

Deobandism remains a powerful player throughout South Asia today, and its power is spreading. Deobandi madrassas in Pakistan spawned both the Taleban movement in Afghanistan and the many

Taleban-style Sunni extremist groups that continue to trouble Pakistani society; Deobandism has also converted a large percentage of the Pakistani Army's officer class, once a bastion of Western-style secularism, and has increasingly gained control of the Moslem separatist movement in Indian-controlled Kashmir. Pakistan's founders envisioned a secular nation, with equal rights for Sunnis, Shi'as, and the small Christian minority; today, life in Pakistan is increasingly dominated by Sunni fundamentalists, who terrorize the country's Shi'as, Christians, and moderate and secular-minded Sunnis. The secular education system has broken down, leaving hundreds of Saudi-funded fundamentalist madrassas to churn out millions of graduates who can quote the Koran from memory, fire a Kalashnikov, and do little else.

Egypt is another country where European colonialism helped radicalize large numbers of Moslems, and attract them to a variation of al-Taymiyya's Salafism. In 1938, a theologian, philosopher, and political theorist named Hasan al-Banna founded the Egyptian version of the Moslem Brotherhood, at least partially in reaction to British domination of Egypt and the power wielded by Christian Europeans in the country. From its very beginnings, the Egyptian Ikhwan's beliefs have had a strong racist element. German historians have recently discovered that al-Banna received financial help and schooling in propaganda from the Nazis, including financing for a printing press and help in disseminating Arabic translations of *Mein Kampf* and *The Protocols of the Elders of Zion* across the Middle East. During the Second World War, Brotherhood members supported a German-Italian victory over the Allies in North Africa. It is hard to blame them: tens of thousands of Moslem colonial subjects from North Africa and present-day India and Pakistan died fighting for their British and French rulers in both the First and Second World Wars and were rewarded with continued discrimination and exploitation: one of the great untold stories of injustice of the twentieth century; no Tom Brokaw has written a *Greatest Generation* praising them.

By the time Egypt won its independence in 1953, a virtual state of war existed between the Brotherhood and the Egyptian colonial regime, assassinations on one side and executions and extrajudicial killings on the other. Al-Banna himself had been murdered in 1949, almost certainly by Egyptian security agents in retaliation for the Brotherhood's assassination of Prime Minister Nokrashi of the puppet colonial government in Cairo. He was succeeded as the Ikhwan's head by Syed Qutb, who was attending college in the United States at the time of al-Banna's death; Qutb continued the Brotherhood's war against secular authority, now in the form of Gamal Abdel Nasser's independent Egyptian republic, until he was arrested for treason and executed in 1966.

Both al-Banna and Qutb are much praised by today's Salafists for their supposed scholarship, but I must admit that their writings leave me cold in comparison to the Koran, al-Taymiyya's acerbic writings, the great Shi'a classic the *Najul Balagha*, or bin Laden's poetry, for example. Especially Qutb: his polemic about his experiences in this country, titled *What I Saw in America*, that is still read by radical Sunnis as an accurate picture of life in the decadent West, is so uniformly awful that one is tempted to retitle it *What I Imagined I Saw in America: Confessions of a Dirty Young Man.*

Qutb seems to have spent his whole time in America in a state of acute sexual excitement, frustration, and rage. Here he is on American women: "The American girl is well acquainted with her body's seductive capacity, and knows it lies in the face, and in the expressive eyes, and thirsty lips, and in the round buttocks, and in the shapely thighs . . . [and] sleek legs . . . and she knows this and does not hide it." The male counterparts of these temptresses were subhuman brutes with "wide strapping chests" and "ox muscles," and the two sexes cavorted to the accompaniment of jazz, of which Qutb has nothing good to say either: it was invented by "the savage bushmen" [sic], "to accompany their primitive dance"; no wonder, then, that jazz singing reminded Qutb of "crude screaming" (Billie Holliday? Ella Fitzgerald?).

It all came together for Qutb at a party he attended: "The dance floor was replete with tapping feet, entwining legs, arms wrapped around waists, lips pressed to lips and chests pressed to chests. The atmosphere was full of desire." By the way, Qutb wasn't writing about Greenwich Village or Hollywood; he spent his brief time in America attending a teacher's college in Greeley, Colorado, a town in which bars and liquor stores were banned, and the dance he described so feverishly was a church social! When you see photographs of Qutb, the reasons for the spite behind his writing become all too obvious: he was grotesquely ugly, almost cartoon-like, with a physiognomy very much like that of Mr. Toad of Toad Hall.

The war between the Egyptian state and the Brotherhood didn't end with Qutb's death on the gallows. Anwar Sadat was killed in 1981 by members of the Ikhwan who had infiltrated the Egyptian Army, and his successor, Hosni Mubarak, has been the target of several Brotherhood assassination attempts. For their part, the Egyptian authorities have imprisoned, tortured, and executed hundreds of Ikhwan members and supporters. Today the Egyptian Ikhwan is split between more moderate members who seek power through the ballot box and unreconstructed radicals who still pursue a violent path, including mountain attacks on foreign tourists, Egyptian Coptic Christians, and anyone else they claim are enemies of the "true Islam." In the global arena, the Egyptian Ikhwan has produced such notables as the blind sheikh, Omar Abdul-Rahman, spiritual godfather of the first World Trade Center bombers, and Dr. Ayman al-Zawahiri, second in command to Osama bin Laden in the al-Qaeda hierarchy.

Al-Zawahiri was already an active Moslem Brotherhood member when Sadat was assassinated in 1981, and he was among the hundreds of suspects arrested for possible involvement in the killing. After a lengthy period of imprisonment, during which he was reportedly beaten and tortured with electricity, he was released for lack of evidence. Not surprisingly, he was much more radical after his incarceration.

The problem with so many of our strategies for defeating terrorism, as well as our policies toward Palestine, Chechnya, Kashmir, and other Moslem nations, is that they multiply the numbers of our enemies while doing little effective to counter the terrorist threat: the worst of all possible worlds. It is simply not true that "they hate us because of who we are," as many in our government and media have claimed; they may loathe us, as Syed Qutb did, but the reason they actively hate us enough to kill us is because of our actions, the things that we and our allies do that harm Moslems. Osama bin Laden is on record in no uncertain terms as having been inspired to demolish the Twin Towers when he saw footage of Israeli bulldozers (machines built in the United States) knocking down Palestinian houses in the Gaza Strip, and he has offered truces with the United States and other Western countries in return for troop withdrawals from Iraq and Saudi Arabia and other changes in policy.

As Bob Baer and others have written, al-Qaeda is only the tip of the Salafi iceberg. Wahabbis, Deobandis, Taleban, Moslem Brothers, all of the members of the various Salafi sects have the potential to carry out attacks like those on 9/11. The last thing we should do is swell the ranks of potential terrorists with misguided policies, strategies, and tactics.

The Moslem Brotherhood's basic creed sounds confrontational, aggressive:

Allah is our object.
The Prophet is our leader.
Qu'ran is our law.
Jihad is our way.
Dying in the name of Allah is our highest goal.

But that doesn't make everyone in the Ikhwan a terrorist, a fanatic, or an extremist, or even a supporter of violence against non-Moslems and more moderate members of the faith, any more than every Southern Methodist who sings "Onward Christian Soldiers" is about to strap on a sword and head out to smite unwed mothers and adulterers. Jihad, remember, means "striving for the faith," which can mean a whole range of activities depending on who is invoking it: building child care centers in slum neighborhoods in Lebanon (the Shi'as of Hizbollah), firing rockets into Israel (the same Hizbollah Shi'as), traveling to poorer Moslem countries to repair mosques and build schools (Malaysian Sunnis), forming Rotary Club–like businessmen's charitable groups (moderate members of the Ikhwan from all over the world), or strapping on explosive vests and killing civilians in Iraq, Afghanistan, Israel, and Pakistan (radical members of the Ikhwan from all over the world). The Brotherhood's official website boasts that "The *Ikhwan* has branches in over seventy countries all over the world," and goes on to proclaim proudly that "the . . . movement is flexible enough . . . [to deal with] . . . every country's circumstances."

The Ikhwan, with its countless members and its global network of cells, would seem to be an ideal place to wage the so-called War on Terror; to start joining forces with the moderates in the Brotherhood, who by all evidence are a clear majority, and isolate the extremists, cutting off the flow of members into radical, violent Salafi groups like al-Qaeda. The problem is, we have no real contacts with the Ikhwan, and no governmental institutions capable of dialoguing with it. As former CIA agents like Bob Baer have pointed out, the agency doesn't even know who is in the Ikhwan or how to approach them; the State Department, accustomed to dealing with nations and regimes, has a poor record in dealing with unofficial, extralegal groups, and the U.S. military only interfaces with Brotherhood-type entities in the context of ongoing military campaigns. No wonder we have trouble playing a constructive role in the War Over the Future of Islam.

CHAPTER 3

THE DEVILS' TEAHOUSE

As the war in Afghanistan continued on through the late 1980s into the 1990s, more and more foreign Moslems like the young Saudi began to arrive on the scene. For the world's Salafis, Peshawar, the Pakistani border city east of the Khyber Pass where the Afghan resistance was based, was like Paris in the '30s, during the Spanish Civil War. The influence of their narrow-minded religious fervor became more and more obvious inside the war zone and along the Afghan-Pakistan border.

By this time I was spending five months out of every year in Peshawar. I went into Afghanistan every couple of months to cover the fighting for *Time* magazine, CBS News, and other news venues, and sometimes I brought medical supplies for the *mujahedin* and displaced Afghan civilians.

I shared a series of rented houses with other Western journalists in the University Town section of Peshawar. Groups of Arabs moved into many of the neighboring compounds, and they were uniformly hostile. Some nights they fired at our residences with their Kalashnikovs, volleys of bullets smacking into the concrete walls. We often had Afghan guards living with us, assigned by the various resistance group headquartered in Pakistan, and they shook their heads in disgust when we asked them not to return fire. Many of them wanted to attack the Arab houses in retaliation and slaughter the occupants.

At night, reporters, aid workers, and other Westerners involved in Afghanistan used to gather at Peshawar's American Club for dinner; the club was a ten minute walk from our house, and we often walked home late at night after an evening of dining, drinking (the club had the only bar in town), and trading the latest news out of the war zone. The Arabs used to prowl the streets of University Town in their expensive four-wheel drive Pajeros, and when they saw us walking they would give chase. We treated it like a game, running around corners, ducking down alleys too narrow or vehicles to follow, jumping walls and detouring through construction sites 'til we made it home safely.

Back then, the foreign Moslems seemed like a joke, a cartoonish threat, compared to the Soviets and their Afghan Communist allies. Several of us had been targeted in the past by Khad, the KGB-trained Afghan secret police, for our outspoken reporting on the war. I myself had been threatened by a Soviet diplomat in Islamabad who accused me of being an "American spy," and I had later survived two assassination attempts in the Tribal Area of the North West Frontier Province (a rocket-propelled grenade and a suitcase bomb, both aimed at a bus I was supposed to be on).

Knowing what I know now, we didn't pay nearly enough attention to the way Saudi money and Pakistani machinations were twisting the Afghans' fight for freedom into something ugly and hateful.

Ever since the U.S. and its allies Saudi Arabia, Egypt, and China had begun sending aid to the Afghan resistance, Pakistan had set itself up as the sole intermediary distributing money, weapons, and supplies to the various *mujahedin* groups. The CIA, who administered the aid program, inexplicably stood by while the masterminds of I.S.I., Pakistan's military intelligence establishment, diverted the great majority of aid to Gulbuddin Heckmatyar's Hizb-i-Islami group.

There were six major Pakistan-based *mujahedin* groups, including the progressive, multiethnic Jamiat-i-Islami, the moderate royalists of the National Islamic Front of Afghanistan (NIFA), and more conservative groups like Harakat, Ittehad, Hizbi-i-Islami (Yunis Khales's party), and Hizb-i-Islami (Gulbuddin Heckmatyar's party) whose members were almost all drawn from Afghanistan's dominant Pushtun tribe. Of the six groups, Gulbuddin's was by far the least effective in actually fighting the Soviets; his *mujahedin* spent most of their time fighting rival groups and harassing and assassinating liberal Afghans and Westerners.

In his excellent book *Afghanistan: Inside a Rebel Stronghold*, British reporter Mike Martin writes of visiting a Gulbuddin commander in the mountains of central Afghanistan in 1984, at a time when the Soviets' superior firepower was inflicting huge losses on the *mujahedin* and their civilian supporters all across the country. Under its amiable commander Sher Ali, this particular guerrilla group was doing almost no fighting, till one day he and his men, along with several other Gulbuddin groups, began marching north for a huge offensive. But they weren't going to attack the Soviets or their Afghan Communist allies as Martin first assumed; "They were heading north to join Tooran [the regional chief for Gulbuddin] in his fight against Harakat." Like Hizb-i-Islami (Gulbuddin), Harakat was a predominantly Pushtun group and ultrareligious, but unlike Gulbuddin's group its mostly rural members supported the return of the king, Zair Shah, after the Soviets were defeated. This was enough to make Gulbuddin's central command regard them as deadly enemies, even if most local commanders didn't share their leaders' hostility to their fellow *mujahedin* in Harakat. Martin accompanied the Gulbuddin forces north, across the Mountains of the Broken Teeth into Harakat territory, only to be caught up with them when they were ambushed and forced to hole up in an abandoned mud fort. When the Gulbuddin war party attempted to retreat back to Bamiyan, they were attacked by vastly superior numbers of Harakat *muj* and forced to flee back to the safety of the fort.

"Thus began the siege of Sayghan which went on for several days," Martin writes. There were skirmishes and firefights during the day and major assaults on the fort every night. Food and water grew scarce, and the cigarette supply ran out; finally ". . . a rumor started that Harakat was bringing up a big gun," capable of demolishing the fort's walls. The Gulbuddin commanders were forced to sue for peace, and after prolonged negotiations were allowed to march back over the mountains to Bamiyan and Ghorband, accompanied by a corps of white-robed, long-bearded elders bearing a Koran, to guarantee their safe passage.

I got to see Gulbuddin's minions deliberately obstruct the war against the Soviets many times during the '80s and '90s; loyal servants of ISI, they were less concerned with winning the Jihad than they were with who would rule Afghanistan after the Communists were gone, paradoxical as it may sound. Once, in the late 1980s, I accompanied the NIFA commander Rahim Wardak, now minister of defense for the Karzai regime, as they prepared for an attack on Asadabad, the capital of Kunar Province. The ridgeline border of Pakistan overlooks the Kunar River valley and the only major road connecting Asadabad with the outside world. Wardak and his *mujahedin* cached their stockpiles of BM-1 rockets and heavy mortar shells along the ridge top under tight security; their plan was to unleash a massive barrage on the posts guarding the road, and then attempt to capture the town itself. The key was surprise: to take out the road's defenders when they weren't ready, troops in the open and vehicles laagered tightly together.

A couple of hours before the barrage was due to commence, someone down the forested mountainside opened up on the road with random bursts of 12.7 millimeter machine-gun fire. I went down with a group of NIFA fighters to investigate. We found an outpost of Gulbuddin's men in a sandbagged emplacement in the trees; a burly

machine-gunner was firing blindly down into the valley. When the
NIFA *muj* complained about the premature firing, Gulbuddin's
men only laughed at them. It was already too late: the Russians
and Afghan Communists were beginning to fire back at the mountainside and the ridge with high explosives, up to and including
FROG-7 rockets. I talked to the machine-gunner, and he told me,
in English, that he was a Pakistani; no doubt an ISI man in civilian
clothes, on loan to Gulbuddin's group.

We hiked back up to the ridgetop and the main NIFA emplace-
ments, and watched, on cue, as the bombardment of the Sadabad
road began: hundreds of rockets and shells; but it was already too
late. Warned by the firing of the Gulbuddin machine gun, the
enemy posts had already hunkered down, dispersed their vehicles,
and were continuing to direct counterfire on the NIFA positions.
As the sun began to set and the barrage ebbed, a convoy of Soviet
reinforcements rolled north from Jalalabad to bolster Asadabad's
defenses.

Another time, outside Khost, I was traveling with some of
Jalaluddin Haqqani's men in a pickup truck through the maze of
badlands east of the besieged town. The route to the front lines
wound around, avoiding the exposed ridges where Soviet helicopters and planes might be able to catch one out in the open. We
came up to a notch dominated by a primitive blockhouse with a
heavy machine-gun barrel protruding from a narrow loophole, a barricade consisting of a pole weighted with a concrete block on one

end. When one of Haqqani's men dismounted and went to swing the barricade up, someone inside the blockhouse shouted to us to back up and find another way around, or the machine gun would open fire. Entreaties from Haqqani's men, then threats and curses, all to no avail; we ended up retreating down the steep hill and taking the long way around, along exposed uplands studded with bomb and rocket craters. I asked the pickup driver who the men in the blockhouse were, and he scowled and replied simply "Gulbuddin," with a finger across his throat and a sound imitating a throat being cut. And Haqqani belonged to Hizbi-i-Islami (Yunis Khalis), close ideological allies with Gulbuddin's party.

Typical.

In the late 1980s, Gulbuddin's followers were implicated in the killings of several Western journalists and aid workers and moderate Afghan resistance leaders. On January 10, 1987, a Polish-British filmmaker/journalist, Andy Skrzypkowiak, was on his way out of Afghanistan with footage of Commander Ahmad Shah Massoud's guerrillas in action against the Soviets north of Kabul. Andy, a tough ex-SAS soldier whose mother had been a refugee from the Nazis and Communists, had previously filmed a convoy ambush by Massood's men along the Salang Highway, a documentary that helped make the dashing young Tajik commander famous in the West. Gulbuddin hated Tajiks, Massood in particular, even more than he hated Westerners and other rival *muj*. Andy had been warned about how dangerous the situation inside Afghanistan had become; when he

stopped for the night in a strange village, he insisted on sleeping outside, where he felt he was safer. A group of Gulbuddin's men dropped
a large rock on his head from a rooftop, killing him.

Dr. Bahouddin Majrooh was probably the most important intel-
lectual figure in the Afghan exile community in Pakistan. Elderly,
tall, elegant, a former Kabul University professor, well-traveled, and
fluent in several languages, he ran Peshawar's Afghan Information
Center, the only source for accurate information about the situation inside Afghanistan. Though Majrooh's personal sentiments
were moderate, pro-Western, and secular, he publicized the views
of all the different Afghan factions, including the more traditionally
religious ones. In the winter of 1987–1988, Majrooh conducted a
public opinion poll in the Afghan refugee community in Pakistan
on what form of government the refugees wanted once the Soviets
were gone; when the results showed a clear majority favored the return
of Afghanistan's king, Zair Shah, Majrooh unknowingly signed his
own death warrant, courtesy of Gulbuddin and ISI. Again, Gulbuddin
and his fellow-fundamentalists favored a religious dictatorship in
Afghanistan, not a constitutional monarchy; Majrooh's poll enraged
them; and the last thing ISI wanted was a strong independent
Afghanistan with a popular leader, Zair Shah or anyone else.

On the evening of February 11, 1988, the professor was alone at
the compound in the University Town neighborhood that housed
his residence and offices. When someone rang the bell at his outer
gate, he went to see who it was; as soon as he opened the gate, a lone

gunman shot him point-blank, emptying an entire AK-47 magazine into his body. I was in Peshawar the evening of the assassination: I had just returned from a trip inside Afghanistan, and I was going to check in with Majrooh, who was a close friend of mine; at the last minute, I decided to wait 'til the next morning, after I'd had a few hours of sleep. When someone called the rented house where I and several other reporters lived with the news of his death, I was one of the first few people on the scene, in time to see the big splotch of blood on the gate, still wet: the death scene of the humane, progressive heart of the Afghan jihad.

No one was ever caught and punished for the killings of Andy, Professor Majrooh, or Gulbuddin's other victims. It was common knowledge in Pakistan that Gulbuddin operated with the full approval of ISI, with the CIA behind them, offering tacit approval of everything they did through a cynical, malign air of "What happens in the jihad stays in the jihad." "Green on green violence," the spooks smugly called it, meaning "Moslems killing Moslems." The demons that were to emerge from Afghanistan in September 2001 were sired in the misery of Afghanistan by cologned men in suits and ties in Langley, Virginia, on Capitol Hill and in the White House.

Gulbuddin and his cohorts had many dark sides. In one incident, he promised safe passage to a large group of Massood's top subcommanders, who needed to pass through Gulbuddin-controlled territory east of Kabul to attend a conference of Jamiat-i-Islami commanders. When Massood's men were passing through Soroobi, the Gulbuddin commander there detained them and tortured them all to death. Years later, Gulbuddin himself was temporarily jailed in Peshawar, and after he was released a photograph circulated of him enthusiastically performing fellatio on one of his Pakistani jailers. Gulbuddin eventually tracked down the joker who was passing out copies of the photo, and the man's severed head turned up in burlap bag in the Kabul River, on the outskirts of Peshawar.

Again, this was the man who received the lion's share of CIA aid to the Afghan resistance, thanks to the machinations of ISI. Meanwhile, the most effective anti-Soviet guerrilla commander, Ahmad Shah Massoud, was consistently undersupplied by the Pakistani military. In at least one case, ISI attempted to assassinate Massood: a truckload of arms and ammunition, sent in by ISI, was supposed to be personally inspected by the Tajik leader upon its arrival. Luckily Massood was somewhere else when it arrived at his headquarters in the ipper Panjshir Valley: the truck had been booby- trapped, and it exploded as it was being unloaded, killing over forty *mujahedin*. It was no wonder that Massood was the only prominent resistance leader, aside from those of the Hazaras, who never once visited Pakistan during the war; I stayed with Massood's father in Peshawar for a couple of weeks during the 1990s, and the old man told me that his son was positive the ISI and/or Gulbuddin would kill him as soon as he arrived in Peshawar.

Though neither I nor any of the journalists I knew realized it at the time, Osama bin Laden and his followers among the Arabs and

other foreign Moslems were already establishing ties with Gulbuddin
and some of the other Moslem extremists in Afghanistan, and taking a more and more active part in the fighting against the Russians.
It was at this time that bin Laden's intense emotional attachment
to Afghanistan began, that he began to develop his Rousseauian
view of the Afghans as simple, pure-hearted, courageous mountain
people.[1] The way the Afghans, one of the poorest nations on earth,
stood up to the Soviet superpower inspired bin Laden's whole idea
of global jihad and how it would eventually prevail. At the same
time, he and his Arabs' behavior toward the Afghans was all too
often condescending, and the Afghans responded to it with anger
and scorn.

Afghanistan is where bin Laden came of age, discovered himself;
where the callow, naïve young Saudi, regarded by most Afghans as a
source of money and nothing more, began the process of becoming
the Sheikh, the Prophet on the White Horse, handing out *fatwas*[2]

---

[1] Bin Laden made the same mistake that most Westerners writing about
Afghanistan make: mistaking Afghanistan's economic poverty, high illiteracy rate,
and tribalism for proof that the country is "primitive." In reality, Afghanistan has
been the site of many of the richest, most sophisticated civilizations in history.
Just one example: Hakim Sanai, Afghanistan's great Sufi poet, actually *taught* the
legendary Rumi to be a poet. Millions of Afghans, truck drivers, peasants, and
beggars, can quote his poems, thousands of lines, by memory. In contrast were the
Saudis, who aside from the Koran produced little more than tents, mud huts, and
epistolary verses to camels during their long history.

[2] A *fatwa* or religious edict gives permission to Moslems to legally take an action
hitherto considerd to be illegal or immoral. In bin Laden's case, this has included
giving approval to actions that kill Christian and Jewish noncombatants, or that
inadvertently cause the deaths of innocent Moslems during attacks on enemies of

left and right and setting himself up as head of an organization with pretenses to being a superpower, able to mount military operations worldwide and demanding to negotiate as an equal with the United States and other industrial and military powers.

It was a hit-and-miss process—as late as 1991 bin Laden contributed a million and a half dollars toward a totally spurious "plan" by some greedy *mujahedin* to attack and capture Kabul; the money vanished, and the attack on Kabul never materialized.

And it also had its cold, cynical side. In the spring of 1987, bin Laden and his Arabs claimed a major victory over the Soviets and Afghan Communists at Jaji, on the main guerrilla supply route from Terri Mangal to Jalalabad and Kabul. Operating from a base they called "Masada" or "the Lion's Den," they supposedly repelled an attack by Soviet Spetznatz (Special Forces) troops, backed by massive airpower, inflicting heavy losses on the enemy.

News of the battle was publicized throughout the Moslem world by the jihadi press, which claimed, among other things, that few or no Afghans were involved in the fighting. Interestingly, one piece, in the Saudi magazine *Al Majallah*, is totally contradictory: "During this bitter campaign some seventy Afghan Mujahedeen and thirteen [Arab] supporters fell martyrs."

Islam. Fatwas are only supposed to be issued by recognized religious authorities, based on sources in the Koran or Hadith. Bin Laden has been severely criticized by many Moslem theologians, including fellow Salafis, for his reckless and theologically weak *fatwas*.

The foreign jihadis' accounts of the fighting at Jaji make amusing reading to anyone who spent time with the Afghan resistance in the Safed Koh, where Jaji is located. "The snow was covering the earth face, and the *mujahedin* could not even see the snow at midday because of the cold," *Jihad Magazine* breathlessly reported. "They were putting water in plastic bottles and would wake up and see them frozen." Another visitor, a Syrian, wrote, ". . . I saw things that by God I have never seen before. A Soviet airplane, a MiG I believe . . . broke to pieces as it fell in front of our eyes." To quote a young Palestinian, "the airplanes were dropping bombs . . . [containing] napalm. One and a half tons of bombs, every five or ten seconds."

As someone who spent time around Jaji from 1984 on, the actual fighting the magazine breathlessly described sounded remarkably similar to many inconclusive battles in the Jaji area during the war, and the weather was typical of a Hindu Kush winter.

The Afghans did most of the actual fighting, and the end result was a draw: the Soviets and Afghan Communists still held their firebase near Jaji Khel, from which they continued to harass *mujahedin* fighters and supply caravans traveling into the interior of Afghanistan; the fighting there continued on for years after the "Battle of the Lion's Den."

Interestingly, it was about this time that bin Laden began to break away from his mentor, the Palestinian leader Abdullah Azzam. Up until then, Osama had accepted Azzam's spiritual, political, and strategic guidance, but after meeting the Egyptian Dr. Ayman al-Zawahiri, his views toward the Afghan jihad began to radically change. Unlike al-Zawahiri, Azzam genuinely cared about the Afghans' struggle on its own terms, regardless of theological differences within Islam. In 1988 and 1989 Azzam made two perilous journeys to the Panjshir Valley, fourteen days each way over passes up to 16,000 feet above sea level, to visit Ahmad Shah Massood; he was so impressed by the Tajik leader that he wrote a book about him called *One Month Among the Giants*. One of Azzam's companions described Massood as "greater than Napoleon."

Compared to Azzam, bin Laden's participation in the Afghan jihad was almost like that of a tourist: he never traveled more than a day or two from the Pakistan border, and despite his overblown claims of heroism at Jaji most of his time was spent safely behind the battle-lines, building roads, air raid shelters, and such. His activities could be plainly seen north of Jaji, where he was bulldozing an improved road to the front far to the north, around Jegdeleg, and at border-hugging locales east of Jaji, where he blasted air raid shelters and other subterranean installations out of the rock.

I think I remember seeing him once, on the hill above Azrow, at dusk: a tall figure, driving a big yellow earth-mover, scraping out another section of switchback. I was alone, carrying an enormous pack, groggy with dengue fever, headed toward Jaji, and in my dusty Afghan clothes I must have looked like just another local Pushtun; we may have even traded "Asalaam aleikums" as I trudged past him into the village. A half hour before that, just after my guide had ridden away after a confrontation involving a knife he was carrying and a large rock I picked up off the ground, I had passed scores of foreign Moslem fighters, mostly Sudanese, traveling north, the way I had come; they were on a section of trail twenty feet or so above me, it was very nearly dark, and they too had mistaken me for a local; Western journalists just didn't travel alone in Afghanistan, especially after dark. I had exchanged greetings with them, too, vaguely conscious in my fevered haze that if they knew who I was, I would have been shot or had my throat cut within seconds.

Al-Zawahiri, like many of his fellow Egyptians, had become an adherent of *takfir*, the Salafists' intolerant doctrine of declaring Moslems they disagreed with apostates, as bad or worse than heretics. This fit in well with the Deobandi faith of many ISI officers, and with Gulbuddin's hatred of anything secular, modern, or Western. He and Gulbuddin, neither with the support of bin Laden, began to intrigue against Azzam in Peshawar, spreading rumors that he wasn't a good Moslem or a loyal Jihadi.

Events followed quickly after that. In April 1988, Azzam first used the word al-Qaeda, "the Base," when he wrote about the necessity of a strong support center for the Islamic struggle in an article in *Jihad Magazine*; Azzam's vision stressed education and training as much as fighting, and was concerned about the quality of jihadi recruits over sheer numbers. Four months later, bin Laden launched his own version of al-Qaeda, focusing on military action; even when many of his closest Arab followers were killed in suicidal attacks on fortified positions over open ground during the abortive siege of Jalalabad in the summer of 1989, he never changed his position. Conveniently, Azzam died less than two months after bin Laden launched his rival group.

I spent a couple of days at the front during the Jalalabad fighting, and it was an idiotic offensive from start to finish. Guerrilla fighters lose whatever advantage they have when they either set up immobile defensive positions or attack the same; in either case, their lack of heavy weapons and air cover inevitably proves fatal. I recall hiding out in an abandoned concrete building while Sukhoi jets leisurely circled above, popping flares to divert surface-to-air missiles and dropping cluster bombs and firing rockets whenever they caught groups of *mujahedin* out in the open. Many members of the inner circle of Masada veterans died in the fighting; bin Laden reportedly wept when he heard of the losses among his Arab followers, but then he was nowhere near the front lines, discretely staying well in the rear.

I also remember the amount of energy Osama's Arabs wasted threatening Western journalists, most of whom like me had been with the *mujahedin* long before bin Laden and his followers showed up on the scene in force. Crossing the border with a group of Jamiat guerrillas at Torkham Khyber, I attracted the attention of a busload of Arabs, who aimed their Kalashnikovs at me and began dry-sniping, pulling the triggers with the safeties on; this unwanted activity infuriated my Afghan companions, who trumped the Arabs by pointing

RPG-7 grenade launchers at their vehicle and threatening to blow it and them sky-high. When the Arabs' bus rapidly pulled away, the *muj* jeered at their fleeing foes with their favorite epithets, "donkey people" and "sister-fucker".

I was not the only journalist harassed by the increasingly xenophobic bin Laden and company at Jalalabad. Eddie Girardet, the veteran *Christian Science Monitor* correspondent, was threatened by bin Laden himself, who told him, "This is our jihad not your jihad" and "If you ever come again, I'll kill you." *National Geographic* photographer Steve McCurry, who had been covering Afghanistan since way back in '79, had a similar confrontation. Another reporter, an Englishman, was with some *mujahedin* friends when they encountered bin Laden; Osama ordered the Afghans to shoot their "infidel" companion, and when they refused he reportedly fell flat weeping and pounding his fists on the ground. Incidentally, I am not retelling this story to amuse: it is another piece in the puzzle, the picture of just how dangerous bin Laden is; most truly destructive men are motivated in part by some kind of strange weakness or delusion.

Bin Laden himself wasn't in Peshawar on November 24, 1989, when Abdullah Azzam and two of his sons were killed; the car they were in was struck by a remote-controlled mine armed with twenty kilograms of high explosives. There were many suspects in the assassination: the Afghan Communists' KGB-style security agency, KHAD; ISI; the CIA; Gulbuddin; Zawahiri's Egyptian

Salafists (who for some time had been accusing Azzam of being a U.S. agent), even Mossad. Strangely, very few fingers were pointed to Osama himself.

I've thought about it for a long time, and I have to say that, though his motives were extremely strong, his hunger for power and his desire to expand on his newfound fame boundless, I'm not sure I believe that Osama was the prime mover behind the killing of his one-time mentor. I'm pretty sure that Gulbuddin was the guilty party, aided and abetted by ISI, with Zawahiri's Egptians as co-conspirators. If Azzam had succeeded in allying the foreign Salafists with Commander Massood, that would have been a disaster for Gulbuddin and his Pakistani puppet-masters, and a slap in the face for Zawahiri; and if bin Laden had financially supported Azzam in favor of Zawahiri, the Egyptian and his followers would have been hard-pressed financially to pursue their version of the jihad.

What is clear, though, is that bin Laden must have known who did it as soon as it happened, perhaps even before the fact; and he either did nothing to stop it, or at least didn't hesitate to benefit from his old friend's death. If he was so attached to his self-appointed role as guardian of the Afghan jihad that he wanted to kill the few Western journalists who dared to cover it—most of whom, inciden-tally, had rendered invaluable assistance to the *mujahedin* by publi-cizing their struggle back when nobody, including Osama, was even noticing it—then how much more intolerable must it have been to have to share the spotlight with Abdullah Azzam, a man with ten times Osama's courage and endurance, and an ability to bond with mainstream Afghans that bin Laden would never understand?

Looking at things dispassionately, one can perhaps forgive bin Laden's rage at the West and even, to some point, the actions it inspired, but his at best equivocal role in Abdullah Azzam's death, and his willingness to leap into the arms of his friend's killers, is absolutely evil, ugly, reprehensible. And it foreshadows much worse to come, in the way of crimes and outrages against his fellow Moslems.

While it is true that the jihad, Salafism, and al-Qaeda itself would go on after bin Laden's death, it is also true that he is a uniquely dangerous enemy, a man with an almost infinitely varied set of talents and skills. There is something uncanny about the soft-spoken, cold-blooded, preternaturally brilliant man, who vanished from our grasp seven years ago after committing one of the greatest crimes in history and hasn't been seen since.

At one time or another, depending on whom you listen to, bin Laden has been a world-class volleyball player; an expert equestrian; a brilliant engineer, who has singlehandedly designed and built roads and subterranean air-raid shelters and fortifications, and who has reportedly developed revolutionary new tunneling techniques that leave no trace on the surface; a business genius, who even made money with the shell companies he set up to provide cover for his training camps in the Sudan and the embassy bombing plots in east Africa; one of the great classical Arabic poets of the last several hundred years; a master accountant, who on his own uncovered how the government of the Kingdom of Saudi Arabia was being swindled by its Western oil customers and in turn was misappropriating tens of billions of its income from oil sales; a pioneer in desert agronomy, who worked on developing new kinds of dryland crops in the Sudan and crossbred different strains of *Papaver somniferum* (opium poppies) in Afghanistan to produce unprecedented yields of morphine; a Harvard Business School–class entrepeneur, who applied modern principles of franchising, personnel recruiting and training, and compartmentalized organization to the development of a religious/political movement; an ultra-charismatic figure, who succeeded in turning himself into a brand name with instantaneous recognition everywhere on earth; and a great military tactician in the tradition of Sun Tzu, the first to wage a successful campaign of genuine asymetrical warfare.

CHAPTER 4

ENCOUNTERS WITH
A WARLORD

Somewhere in my office are three or four small color photographs of two handsome young Pushtun men—boys, really—wearing *shalwar kameezes*, carrying small short-barreled Soviet AKMS-47 assault rifles, the kind favored by Russian pilots and commandos and important *mujahedin* commanders. They are buying oranges in a bazaar on the outskirts of Khost, in far eastern Afghanistan.

I took the photos in 1991, a few weeks after the boys' father, Jalaluddin Haqqani, captured Khost, the first major Afghan town to fall to the *mujahedin*. As I remember, their names were Siraj and Nasruddin; I think one of them is dead, killed in a U.S. bombing raid, while the other is somewhere in the border mountains of South Waziristan with his father, fighting alongside bin Laden and al-Qaeda against the United States, its allies, and the Karzai regime.

Most Western journalists didn't like visiting Haqqani very much; he was one of most effective guerrilla commanders in Afghanistan, a classic Pushtun tribal chief, personally courageous and a brilliant field commander, but he had surrounded himself with Arabs and other radical foreign Moslems who hated Westerners; these angry young holy warriors would soon become the first wave of al-Qaeda fighters. More than one correspondent had been beaten up and thrown out of Haqqani's palatial compound in the border town of Miram Shah. For some reason, I had always liked Haqqani, and the old man seemed to have a certain amount of respect for me, probably because I was one of the few journalists who had covered the war for years, stubbornly refusing to quit, and because I was motivated by affection for the Afghans and their cause instead of money or career. I realized later that he had his sons accompany me that day as a kind of insurance, to warn off any of his fanatical foreign supporters who might want to toss a grenade my way or fire a clip of AK-47 slugs into the *kfir*.

Visiting Haqqani was always an exercise in discomfort, danger, and general weirdness. There were only two ways to get from Peshawar to Miram Shah: a big crowded lumbering bus, slow as a sick camel, or the Flying Coaches, van-like minibuses driven by hash- and heroin-smoking drivers who passed on blind curves, road-raced each other (trying to run the rival vehicle off the road was considered 100 percent cricket), and drove 85 miles per hour on bald tires with loose steering and defunct brakes. Almost every day there was a horrendous wreck, with an FC plummeting into a ravine and exploding into flames, killing everyone on board. I always considered that part of the trip at least as hazardous as being on the battlefield inside Afghanistan. Miram Shah lay in a remote part of the FATA, the Federally Administered Tribal Area, a long drive through Darra Adam Khel, where the bazaar featured hashish, opium, and weapons ranging from locally built imitation Kalashnikovs to single-shot .22 caliber assassin's guns disguised as ballpoint pens to big, tan Italian antitank mines and surface-to-air missiles; over Kohat Pass, where the steep stony slopes were littered with the debris from a hundred car and bus wrecks; through Hangu, where firefights between feuding tribesmen were not uncommon; and south across wastelands of jejune desert and dry nullahs choked with rocks and dust.

When you finally pulled up at the bus station in Miram Shah, there was always the same beautifully appropriate greeter: a gibbering madman-cum-village idiot, who welcomed every arriving van and bus and bade farewell to every departing vehicle with the same leaping and whooping. From the terminal, you caught a three-wheeled pedicab to Haqqani's palatial high-walled residence. Haqqani's *marcaz* or base was two or three hours further east, in a deep gorge a few miles short of the embattled town of Khost. (After he captured Khost in March 1991, he moved his headquarters to the mountains beyond; from there, he laid siege to another major town, Gardez.)

Visiting Haqqani's mixed force of local *muj* and young extremists from all over the Moslem world and beyond gave one a priceless closeup view of the uneasy relationship between Afghans and non-Afghans in the jihad. Haqqani's central base for his siege of Khost was a collection of adobe buildings in a deep gorge east of the town; the landscape looked almost exactly like the canyon country of southeastern Utah. The cliff face was a warren of tunnels and shafts, built by none other than bin Laden, I found out later; several contained battered old Soviet T-51 and T-62 tanks, captured by the U.S. in Desert Storm and shipped over to the *mujahedin* via ISI to give the guerrillas some artillery capability.

You never knew who you were going to run into at the Haqqani *marcaz*: Arabs, Palestinians, North Africans, Chinese Moslems from Sinkiang, Kashmiris, even a few non-Moslem Sikhs, sent there by ISI to prepare for guerrilla warfare inside India. The local Afghan *mujahedin* were predictably friendly, as were some of the foreign Moslems, most notably the Palestinians, most of whom spoke perfect English and wanted to chat up Western reporters about pop culture, the current hipness rating of Michael Jackson, how dead disco was, the possibility of *Star Wars* sequels, et al. The Arabs and most of the other "Moslem Foreign Legionnaires" were as hostile as a basket of pit vipers.

On one visit there, the Haqqani fighters in a nearby emplacement outside the canyon bombarded Khost itself with an Egyptian Sakr-20 rocket launcher (a Sakr is a Thunderbolt; twenty refers to its twenty kilometer range); I watched them fire off one six-foot-long projectiles after another; they zipped over the horizon, and a forward observer provided a running commentary on the results: "The last one hit the corner of the jail, and the prisoners are escaping!" Cries of "*Mujahedin Zindabad! Shurovee mortabad!*" from the rocketeers (*shurovee* was a pejorative Afghan term for Russians).

Predictably the *shurovee* were not amused, and that night they mounted a major air attack on the area. Jets circled overhead, dropping bomb after bomb. Everyone headed for the air-raid shelters, but when I tried to enter the Arabs said, "No, we don't want the unclean *kfir* in here with us. The Afghans started to protest, but I said, "Hey, if you don't want me in here with you, I don't want to be in there with you either." I spread out my sleeping bag on an adjacent rooftop, and a few minutes later most of the Afghans in the shelter climbed out and joined me. We spent the night out there as the bombs went off all around, the Afghans occasionally yelling down to the Arabs about what cowards they were compared to the *farranji*, who wasn't afraid of numbs and didn't hide underground. When I actually fell asleep, my status went up several more notches; the truth was, I was dog-tired from several days out in the sun, banging around in a gutsprung pickup, dealing with scowling Arabs and homicidal Communist airmen.

A couple of days later a flash flood swept down the canyon floor above; whenever that happened, mines from the old Soviet minefields washed out into the road and had to be cleared away. The *muj* got ahold of a barely functioning truck and prevailed on a bunch of Arabs to drive it up to the front lines. It lurched away up-canyon and disappeared, the Afghans watching with barely suppressed grins. A couple of minutes later a huge explosion echoed down the gorge. One of the *muj* went to investigate, and came back trying to keep a straight face. "I have bad news and good news," he said in English. "Bad news is, a big truck just blew up. Good news is, it was full of Arabs."

Even Haqqani himself had limited patience with his Arab fans. A guerrilla cameraman had shot a remarkable video of Haqqani leading a group of guerrillas through a deep forest. There was a sudden explosion, either a light mortar round or, more likely, an anti-personnel mine, and the video cut to Haqqani with a big splinter of shrapnel buried in his calf. A Saudi "medic"—every other Arab you met claimed to be a doctor—was attempting to inject a local anesthetic so he could cut it out. He was using the biggest needle I have ever seen used on a human being, a regular horse syringe, and he poked Haqqani again and again, trying unsuccessfully to complete the injection. Finally Haqqani fixed him with his hard eyes and said, "If you don't make it work this time, I'm going to kill you." Somehow, his hands shaking, the terrified Saudi punched the anesthetic into Haqqani's leg.

The old man's Afghan fighters loved the video.

•   •   •

The photographs of Haqqani's two sons were taken on my next and last visit to Haqqani, in the early spring of 1992; he had just captured Khost, the first major town to fall to the resistance, and was besieging Gardez, another important point on the road down to Kabul.

In February 1989, the Soviets had pulled their troops out of Afghanistan, leaving behind a few thousand pilots, advisors, and such. Many people both outside and within Afghanistan predicted this would lead to a rapid victory by the *mujahedin*, but the current Afghan Communist leader in Kabul, ex-KHAD chief Mohammed Najibullah, proved to be a tough nut to crack. In March to April 1989, the *mujahedin* and bin Laden's Arabs mounted their ill-fated siege of Jalalabad, which resulted in massive casualties and little change in the tactical situation in eastern Afghanistan. When I visited Haqqani three years later, it seemed like the war might go on forever; but events were already in motion that were to bring the end of the Najibullah regime and the final end of the Communist adventure in Afghanistan. Interestingly, none of it had anything to do with the machinations of bin Laden, Gulbuddin, ISI, and company.

It happened like this: Najibullah had been depending on Uzbek mercenaries from northern Afghanistan, under General Dostam, to shore up his military forces. Though they were based around Mazar-i-Sharif, in the Uzbek heartland along the Uzbekistan-Tajikistan border, Najibullah airlifted them to every key battle zone where the outcome was in doubt. Even in Gardez, Haqqani's most serious challenge was defeating these fierce, stubborn descendants of the Huns and other Central Asian raiders. One of Haqqani's commanders described how difficult the Uzbeks were to subdue, with something between exasperation and admiration: "We had this one Uzbek tank surrounded, and they were out of fuel and ammunition. We had men on top of the tank with grenades, and we told them to surrender or we would kill them. They told us to fuck our sisters, to go ahead and kill them, they didn't care. We asked then again and again, but they just cursed at us. Finally we pried the hatch open and tossed in grenades. They all died, cursing us to the end."

At one point I was scoping out the Uzbek positions around Gardez through a high-powered spotting scope, from Brigadier Afghani's command post. The brigadier was a flamboyantly mustachioed old character who boasted of having trained with both the British SAS and the Soviet Spetznatz. As I swept the enemy lines, I suddenly found myself backtracking. There was a group of Uzbeks, all of them grinning broadly; one was looking back at me through the exact same kind of scope I was using, while another was carefully sighting in on me with a Sakr-20 rocket launcher. A moment later, there was a big puff of white smoke from the muzzle as he opened fire. I rapidly abandoned my post and took cover in the rocks, and a few moments later the ridgeline to my right exploded in a cloud of dust and vaporized stone.

To get back to the subject at hand, the Soviets had been steadily cutting back in their funding for Najibullah, leaving him unable to pay the Uzbek militias who kept order along the major roads in the north. To make ends meet, the Uzbeks turned highway robber, looting passersbys in trucks and cars. The always-wily commander Massood approached General Dostam covertly, and in April 1992 the two forces, Massood's Tajiks and Dostam's Uzbeks, marched on Kabul from the north.

Immediately Gulbuddin and the Ittehad Party's leader Abdul Rosul Sayaf, along with bin Laden's Arabs, made their own move from the east and south to seize the capital, with the Shi'a Hazaras, backed by Iran approaching from the west, intent on protecting their fellow-tribesmen living in Kabul. The Communist forces melted away, and Najibullah took refuge in the United Nations compound in Kabul.

For the next two years, Kabul became a battleground, fought over by opposing ethnic and political forces, with Pakistan, Saudi Arabia, and Iran pouring in weaponry to their respective surrogates; the United States, which had promised the *mujahedin* they would help safeguard and build a stable government in postwar Afghanistan, stood by and did nothing. Civilians were massacred, and whole neighborhoods literally leveled by house-to-house fighting. By 1995, the remains of the city were controlled by Massood and an ever-changing series of allies. For all his faults, Massood was a genuine nationalist, not controlled by Pakistan, Iran, or anyone else, but he was forced to continue to ally himself with questionable characters like Dostam and Ittehad's Sayaf. Huge numbers of Kabul's Hazaras were either dead or refugees in the Bamiyan Valley, the Hazara heartland, victims of ethnic cleansing by either Massood's Tajiks or the Pushtuns and foreign fighters of Sayaf and Gulbuddin Heckmatyar.

Gulbuddin, Pakistan's proxy in Afghanistan, was one of the big losers in the internecine fighting, and that was intolerable to the ISI

They and their Arab allies were already preparing an alternative: in the refugee camps around Quetta, in western Pakistan, they were organizing a proxy invasion force of Afghan war orphans and mercenaries under the name Taleban, or "religious students." In November 1994, the Taleban made their first appearance, liberating a Pakistani truck convoy bound for Turkmenistan to trade; they were aided by ISI troops and Pakistani "volunteers." By early 1995 they had captured three southern Afghan provinces, including the old capital city of Kandahar, and had been reinforced by nearly fifteen hundred Pakistani Taleban fighters from the Saudi-funded Deobandi *madrassas* that were springing up all over the countryside. On September 26, 1996, after months of bloody fighting, the Taleban captured Kabul, and executed Najibullag a day later, castrating him before hanging him from a light pole in the center of Kabul.

CHAPTER 5

WELCOME TO PARADISE

In the winter of 1996–97, I got the chance to get to know some Salafis—a whole lot of them, in fact, and all too well. I returned to Taleban-ruled Afghanistan via Peshawar, which was now virtually controlled by Afghan Taleban members, their fundamentalist Pakistani allies (who would eventually become Pakistani Taleban), and foreign Moslems led by bin Laden and company.

I hadn't been in Afghanistan for two or three years; I had missed Najibullah's downfall, the brutal *mujahed*-on-*mujahed* fighting that had destroyed most of Kabul, the appearance of the Pakistan-backed Taleban on the scene, the seesaw warfare between Taleban and Massood's Tajiks and his allies, and finally Taleban's capture of the capital, aided by al-Qaeda's "Moslem Foreign Legion" and arms, advisors, and Pakistani "volunteers" provided by ISI Massood and his allies, who now included the Hazaras, were now organized into something called the Northern Alliance; they held most of the country north of Kabul, but the rest of the country was under the control

of the Taleban's makeshift regime, which had captured the ruins of
the capital barely two months before.

I had always loved Peshawar; it definitely lived up to the meaning
of its name, "frontier town," with the great plains of the Indian subcontinent stretching away to the east, and to the west the great wall
of the Hindu Kush ("dead Hindu" mountains) with the Khyber
Pass its secret door, and beyond phalanxes of jagged peaks looming
in a perpetual pall of dust, and beyond that the skyscraping deserts and steppes of Central Asia extending all the way to Turkey,
and the gateway to Europe. It was the world's great crossroads,
geographically, culturally, and historically, a place where a thousand brands of exotica came together: Afghans, Sikhs, Persians,
Mongol Hazaras, and Europeans had all gathered here for centuries to trade, fight, spy, and mingle their legends, destinies, and
bloodlines—and like all true border cities it had an air of openness
and inclusiveness; everyone was a stranger here, and thus, in a way,
no one was an outsider.

Now all that was changing; a fanatical line had been drawn in
the sand and you were either on one side of it or the other. And you
had no choice in the matter: you were condemned at birth to be
either a Believer or an Unbeliever, a Musselman or a *kfir* (or, worse,
an apostate or heretic), a brother or an enemy, and never the twain
would meet.

The Taleban seemed to be everywhere, ubiquitous: they were
asserting their will over the Afghan refugee community and everyday

Pakistani life as well, a shadowy omnipresence, an army of Rasputins in their gigantic black turbans and long black beards.

They had taken over the old Afghan Consulate in Peshawar; I took my passport there and applied for a visa. I had visited Afghanistan at least fifteen times since 1984, but always with the *mujahedin*, crossing the border illegally, without documentation. I had always felt welcome as soon as I crossed the frontier: both fighters and civilians were happy that someone, *anyone*, cared about their plight enough to come there. Ironically, now that I was trying to enter the country legally, the welcome mat was gone. The Talebs at the Consulate were unlikely-looking diplomats—tall, lanky, unkempt, and odoriferous, and they made no secret of their dislike for me. I'm sure they already knew all about me from their friends in the ISI: knew that I had been in Afghanistan before with the *mujahedin* and had been one of the major outlets for news about the jihad to the outside world; several of my accounts of Soviet war crimes and human rights violations had been published in *The Washington Post* and the Helsinki Watch book *A Nation Is Dying*. I had naively hoped that that might earn me some affection, or at least respect: after all, the *mujahedin* were fighting the Russians back then, and it was only later that they degenerated into feudal warlordism and were eventually sent packing by Taleban. It turned out the opposite was true: like Gulbuddin, they cared as much—or more—about who ruled postwar Afghanistan as they did about who actually drove the Soviets out of the country. Actually, they didn't like the *mujahedin* at all, presumably because they weren't theologically pure enough, and they liked me, a *kfir* friend of those bad Moslems, even less.

My visa was supposed to be approved overnight, but when I showed up the next day the Talebs told me with ill-disguised glee that they were awaiting approval from the Foreign Ministry in Kabul; if I showed up the next day at noon, it would be ready. Somehow I wasn't surprised when I waited overnight and showed up at twelve o'clock sharp, when the visas were supposed to be issued at the little window in back, only to find it closed and padlocked. Aside from the Pakistani guards outside the gate, the whole place looked deserted. I sat down on one of the dusty gutsprung couches in the waiting room and waited; I waited and waited, and waited some more, until finally, around mid-afternoon, I gave up and went back to my hotel.

While I waited around Peshawar, I hung around with some of my old comrades from the jihad days. One day, an Afghan friend of mine named Raheem and I ran into a bunch of Talebs out in the University Town neighborhood, on the western edge of the city. They were loitering in front of a shabby concrete building that according to the sign in front housed one of the many Taleban/al-Qaeda type offices that had sprung up all over the city: THE ISLAMIC STUDENTS UNION OF AFGHANISTAN. They were scowling at everyone who walked by, and more of them were peering malevolently out of the upstairs windows.

If you didn't know Raheem, you would have sworn he was the King of the Taleban himself. He was big, with a huge tangled silver-streaked beard, long disheveled hair, and wild electric eyes. But appearances were deceiving: he was actually the Afghan equivalent of a hippie, from an upper-class Kabul family, fond of flute playing and hashish smoking, and not interested in religious orthodoxy at all. He moved to Peshawar during the war against the Russians, where he partied with Western journalists, aid workers, and the like, occasionally accompanying the *mujahedin* back across the border as a kind of unofficial morale officer. When the Communist regime fell he returned to his family's house in Kabul, evicted the squatters living there, and began refurnishing the place. He survived the *muj*-on-*muj* fighting that destroyed half the city, but the house was destroyed; he stayed on, camping out in the ruins. Then the Taleban came to town, and Raheem's flute-playing and hashish-huffing quickly ran him afoul of their Committee for the Propagation of Virtue and Suppression of Vice's omnipresent Religious Police. (As in matters of sex, the Taleban were great hypocrites when it came to music and the arts, too; they banned music and videos, but after they were overthrown a huge cache of Indian movie videos and music cassettes was discovered in the palatial Kandahar home of Mullah Omar, the self-righteous Taleban leader.) The goon squad roughed Raheem up, and they took his beloved silver flute, given to him by a European diplomat, and broke it in half; smashed his clay chillum; and confiscated his stash of hashish. "The next time we catch you smoking or playing music, we cut your fingers off," the fat-bellied mullah in charge said, and he meant it.

If Raheem had stayed in Kabul, he would have killed somebody, or been killed; instead, he wisely got a ride to the outskirts of the city, where a friend was taking care of his horse Geronimo; saddled up and rode east, over the mountain trails south of the Khyber Pass; and ended up back in Peshawar, exiled from his homeland yet again.

The Taleban in University Town didn't know what to make of the two of us: they must have thought Raheem was some kind of turn-coat, hanging around with an accursed *kfir* spy of some kind. When we approached and greeted them with polite "asalaam aleikums" they could barely come out with the customary "aleikum saalams" in response; the words stuck in their throats, threatening to choke them. Their faces were clenched into Noh-like masks of disgust, and one spat deliberately at my feet. When I held out my hand each one took it reluctantly, as if I were a leper. Standard Salafi/Taleban behavior: they hated to touch or share food and drink with non-Moslems, and they were just as bad or worse to fellow-Moslems they considered heretics, like Shi'as or more moderate Sunnis.

There is a nasty streak of racism in the Arabian soul, an obsession with bloodlines, purity, and pollution, combined with extreme sectar-ianism, that is totally at odds with Mohammed's spirit of universality and the *ummah's* racial rainbow, and closer in spirit to Hinduism at its worst than anything else. Echoed in Qutb's writings about America and the West, it has found a happy home in Salafism.

Things got even more interesting when I attempted to interview the Peshawar Talebs; after all, I was a journalist, and that's what journalists are supposed to do. The first three I questioned gave the exact same answers.

"What did you do before you joined Taleban?"

"I was a student." (The same answer from all, whether the speaker looked eighteen or forty.)

"Why did you join Taleban?"

"To bring peace back to Afghanistan, and to establish a true Islamic state there." (The exact same words, recited in a monotone.)

"What do you say to people who say Taleban is controlled by Pakistan?"

"All Moslems everywhere have a duty to help their brothers in jihad." (Like a tape recording.)

As I prepared to interview the fourth Taleb, he smirked and pointed to the man next to him. "Ask him, and he will say the same thing, and so will all the rest of us."

Now, Afghans are the world's most supreme rugged individuals; "Ask three Afghans a question and you will get four answers," as the old saying goes. They disdain orthodoxy and conformity. I once witnessed a debate between a village mullah and a young student; the mullah kept coming out with wild assertions that he claimed were quotes from the Koran, until finally the younger man objected: "Mullah-jan, I've read the Holy Koran, and none of what you said is in there." The mullah stroked his beard sententiously, and said, "Well, if it isn't, it should be." To his credit, when everyone laughed, he joined in.

The Taleban were Afghans, but they were like no Afghans I had ever met; in fact, they were unlike any *people* I had ever met anywhere in the world, with the possible exception of Moonies. Whatever the Saudis and Pakistanis had done to the boys and young men in those refugee camp madrassas, they had succeeded in creating a whole new kind of Afghan, a kind of anti-Afghan, cold, humorless, and robotic. They were the latest edition of Stalin's New Soviet Man, of Mao's Red Guards, of the Khmer Rouge's heartless homicidal were-kids: life didn't exist for them before they were converted, or reborn, or brainwashed if you will, and it didn't exist outside of the group; they had been swallowed whole and digested, and spat out again as less than human.

As we departed, the midday call to prayer began, first one voice, then another, and another, rebounding from loudspeakers on minarets across the city. One of the Talebs called out to Raheem, demanding to know why he wasn't stopping to pray, why he was walking away with the infidel, the Unclean One. All of Raheem's resentments boiled over, and he exploded, into one of the crazy riffs he was sometimes prone to: "YOU ARE THE INFIDELS! YOU TAKE MONEY, AMERICAN DOLLARS, FROM THE KING OF THE ARABS, AND GOLD FROM THE PAKISTANIS, WHO ARE ALL HINDUS, AND YOU KISS THEIR HANDS!" I tried to pull him away—I was sure the knives were going to come out any second—but Raheem broke away and continued: "WHY ARE YOU HERE, IN THE CITY OF THE HINDUS? THE TRUE

MUSSELMEN ARE ALL IN THE MOUNTAINS, WHERE I
LIVE! YOU ARE BLIND, YOU UNDERSTAND NOTHING!"
and he broke into a favorite little song of his, provenance unknown,
about the "Sufi hasheesh-smokers of Kunar."

To my amazement, the Talebs were all looking at each other,
wide-eyed, dumbfounded; their Wahhabi indoctrinators had taught
them that the Sufi mystics of their native land were all apostates,
spiritual outlaws, but somewhere deep inside they still believed in
malangs, who lived in graveyards getting stoned and communing
directly with God, and saints who performed miracles, older than
the Holy Koran itself, brothers of al-Khidr, "The Green Man,"
who taught the prophet Abraham himself, and who still walked the
earth, showing himself to believers as a beggar on the trail, a crazy
man singing and dancing in the bazaar. This tall, wild-looking figure, apparently totally unafraid of them, summoned up their most
basic beliefs. "What do you mean, oh Sufi?" one asked. "Talk to us!"
another implored.

But Raheem had made his point; he strode away, not looking back.
And, predictably, the Taleban were hypocrites. Their enemies and
detractors frequently accused the Taleban of pederasty; most of their
hard-core members were from Kandahar, a city that enjoys a reputa-
tion for homosexuality among other Afghans. There are countless
jokes and japes about it. In fact, on my first visit to Afghanistan
in 1972, one of the first Afghans I met, a burly carpet merchant
in Herat, told me one: "You know, we Afghans say that men from

Kandahar are"—he paused, thinking of how to say it—"they are liking boys, not ladies. This man from Kandahar became very angry; he told his friends it wasn't true. So his friends said, we will make a test. First, they tied a bell to his—you know." He indicated the groin area. "Then they told him to sit in a chair in front of a wall. A boy came and put a picture on the wall, of a beautiful lady's face. They listened, but there was no sound from the bell. The boy came and put up a new picture, of a beautiful lady, and you could see her." He gestured to show the neck and shoulders. "They waited, but the bell made no sound. The boy brought a third picture, but while he was putting it on the wall it fell down. So he went to get it"—and he bent down, his bum in the air—"and, DING-DING-DING-DING—" He imitated the rapid ringing of a bell, and laughed uproariously.

Finally my visa was ready, and I went to the consulate to pick it up. On several of my visits there, I had noticed a boy serving tea to the Talebs. He looked to be twelve or thirteen, certainly not much older; he wore thick rouge on his cheeks, kohl on his eyes, and bangled anklets that clattered when he walked.

On the wall of the waiting room there was a grim poster that I had noticed before: a small black and white photograph of a seated figure of a man, bound hand and foot, against the base of a wall; wreathed in a cloud of dust, a huge bulldozer was preparing to push the wall over onto the man. I couldn't read the Pushtun caption, but it obviously proclaimed the virtues of the Taleban and their merciless effort to eradicate any and all "vices" plaguing Afghan society: their penalty for homosexuality was burying the accused alive or pushing a wall over on them, as in the photograph. I had seen the poster several times by now, and it always kindled a sick, nauseous feeling inside me; just looking at it made me feel somehow complicit, for dealing even indirectly with the perpetrators.

I got my passport back; when I looked inside, there was the precious visa, authorizing one visit to the "Islamic Republic of Afghanistan." As I stepped out into the hall, the tea-boy raced past me, his bare feet slapping on the floor, anklets ringing; he was looking back over his shoulder with a simpering smile on his face at an ungainly, stork-like Taleb who was in hot pursuit, a lascivious smile on his face. The two figures vanished around a corner, and a moment later I heard a door slam behind them.

• • •

If Talebanized Peshawar was strange, actually crossing into the Taleban's Afghanistan was like passing through the looking glass into a Never-Never Nightmare Land.

Another journalist and I hired a car to drive us across the Khyber Pass to the border at Torkham. We showed our visas to the Taleban guards at the gate, who squinted at them upside down and sideways, totally baffled; they finally directed us to a sly-looking plump mullah type, who stamped us officially into the country. Two burly brothers with a van offered to drive us to Kabul for a hundred dollars, and a minute later we were bumping west on the main Peshawar-Kabul highway, or what was left of it. After two decades of fighting, the road had been reduced to a strip of rubble broken by almost continuous craters, some little more than glorified potholes, others big enough to swallow the van whole three times over. Every bridge had been blown up: vehicles had to crawl down steep embankments, crab their way across alluvial boulders and deep sand, and then lurch up the other side. Before the war, Pakistanis used to drive to Kabul for the weekend, or even make a long day of it and go there for lunch and be back in time for dinner; on this day it took us all day, nonstop, to get to Kabul, and when we got there, there was nothing there . . . not a city, anyway.

The fighting between rival *mujahedin* groups had totally destroyed huge areas of Kabul. Mile after mile of the city looked like Berlin or Hiroshima in 1945, like the place had been carpet-bombed, blasted by thousands of heavy artillery pieces and rocket launchers, or nuked. It was hard to believe that the damage had been done by light arms, assault rifles, grenade launchers, and the like. On one street, a concrete wall four feet high, two feet thick, and three or four hundred yards long had been almost completely obliterated by what looked to have been 12.7- or 14.5-millimeter machinegun fire; you could see the individual pockmarks, closer and closer together 'til they virtually gnawed the wall away, into thin air. The impression one got was of a great city devoured by the fires of pure rage.

I had been in Kabul back in the '70s, before the wars, and I still remembered it as a quiet, out-of-time kind of place, walled in by mountains, with green gardens, palaces, parade grounds and playing fields, trolley cars, a fine museum, a zoo—old Central Asia, with a hint of the Balkans, Ruritania. Now it was gone. The trolley cars had been somehow heaped into a huge pile and then set afire and melted together.

In the central traffic circle dividing the north and south sides of the city, an unexploded bomb was stuck in the pavement, half buried. A cigarette vendor sat on it, hawking his wares. Along the skyline to the east towered the skeletons of the parliament and palace, shattered and scorched.

You couldn't blame the Taleban for any of the destruction, though you could definitely assign much of the guilt to the powers behind them, the Pakistanis and Saudi Arabians (the Iranians played their own dirty games on the other side): they had bankrolled Gulbuddin when he did everything in his power to destroy the new *mujahedin* government in Kabul; the destruction of the capital really began when Gulbuddin's forces rained ISI-supplied missiles down on the civilian heart of the city, with no word of protest, by the way, from the U.S.

You would have thought the Taleban, now that they were de facto rulers of Kabul, would have been rebuilding, or if not that, at least *governing*; after all, they were the vanguard of what was supposed to be a new Salafi caliphate, eventually extending all the way from Andalus, ethnically cleansed of Moslems in 1492, to the liberated Islamic states of the Turkomans and Uighurs, and beyond. But no;

quite the opposite, in fact. They seemed content to camp out in the ruins of their new capital, split theological hairs over whether cigarette smoking, *naswar* (snuff), and white socks on women were *hallal* (allowed) or *harram* (forbidden) under sharia law, and maraud through the disintegrating streets in search of wrongdoers to harass. After all, their country's shattered economy, its lack of an educational system, housing, food, potable water, and health care, were of negligible interest when one was laying the foundations of Paradise Lost, God's Kingdom in an age of godless kings and damnable empires.

Their occupation of Kabul was a halfhearted affair; the Taleban were almost all from the rural outback of southern and eastern Afghanistan, places that hadn't changed in centuries until the Soviets invaded in 1979. Their first contact with the twentieth century literally fell on them without warning out of a clear blue sky, in the form of helicopter gunships and jets, bombs and rockets, pain, death, and exile. I remember when I first began interviewing refugees in the camps in Pakistan about the war and how it had impacted their lives: the only English word most of them knew was "bombard," and it occurred again and again in their stories, a sad commentary indeed on "modern times," "progress," "civilization."

George Orwell once wrote that the perfect image for our age was a jackboot kicking someone in the face, over and over and over again; after my first couple of trips into wartime Afghanistan, I saw the present-day world as an endless series of ancient, defenseless, mudwalled villages, burning and exploding, as gunships and MiGs circled above, and the villagers, those who were still alive, streamed from their shattered world. It was no mythopoetic conceit. In 1984, there were still three or four villages between Terri Mangal and Jegdeleg, where a few families stubbornly held fast, trying to farm, sheltering the *mujahedin* when they came through; the rest, 90 percent plus, were totally destroyed and abandoned. A year later, all were gone.

During the jihad years, the cities of Afghanistan were Enemy Territory; the rest of the country, the mountains and deserts, belonged to the *muj*. I recall crossing the highlands of Logar and Ningrahar provinces with the guerrillas, and looking off to the northwest at Kabul, a vast sprawl of darkness on the plains, as remote-seeming as another planet.

The Talebs lived in Kabul like vagrants, street tramps, transients who didn't belong. Here and there a dozen or so fighters bivvied in the wreckage of someone's house; crude encampments with campfires on the concrete driveway were surrounded by trash, furnished with seats torn out of cars; and maybe a battered quad 14.5 heavy machine gun was parked by the curb, its barrels pointed straight up, at nothing. Corpulent mullahs cruised the streets in Pajero SUVs, chauffered by boy-toy drivers in heavy makeup and fingernail polish. Aside from Taleban vehicles, almost all the traffic consisted of bicyclists, horse carts, and men dragging heavy loads on rubber-tired wagons, and there were few of those. In one ruined building that had once been a Hazara command post, locals showed me graffiti left by the fighters: a big heart with "BE MY VALENTINE" written across it in Dari, and next to it the exhortation "Kill Kill Kill everyone you see, so that you may live."

You didn't have to look far to see how astonishingly cruel these moral absolutists could be when faced with human suffering. One of the UN agencies, probably the World Food Program, had a daily food handout for the neediest of the needy; it was held in the early morning, in an empty lot surrounded by crumbling adobe walls. Widows in ragged, patched burkahs, cripples in makeshift wheelchairs, amputees on crutches, tremulous white-bearded ancients lined up in the icy air. A couple of white pickup trucks with United Nations logos drove into the yard, unloaded bags of wheat, and began doling them out, checking them off against a list.

The recipients shuffled forward in long columns. They were too weak and frail to handle the heavy sacks themselves; each had one or more helpers, a companion with a flat-tired wheelbarrow, a couple of children, someone with a tumpline, a rope and a bit of rag. The rope went around the bottom of the sack and was looped over the forehead, with the rag for protection, a simple makeshift load carrier.

There was an indefinable air of anxiety, urgency, about the whole process; both the UN workers and the poor people in line moved quickly. I soon found out why. A few minutes later two trucks full of young Talebs roared into the courtyard. They piled out, and immediately began terrorizing the poor food recipients. Ancient cripples quaked with fear as Talebs surrounded them, shouting and jostling. Women pulled their children close to them, half-cloaking them in their ragged dark burkahs; little kids burst into tears. It was a terrible spectacle. After beating several of the women in the line with rubber hoses, they piled back in their vehicles and roared away.

The thing is, Salafi theology isn't big on human rights, welfare, progress, etc.; they are so focused on theological arcana that the stuff of everyday human life just doesn't rate in their plans. Afghanistan under Taleban and their Wahhabi Arab friends was an interesting test case in what life would be like in a Salafi Paradise; if it resembled anything, it was one of those apocalyptic visions of William Burroughs, *Naked Lunch* or *The Ticket That Exploded*: a wasteland ruled by fanatical brainwashing totalitarians, prowled by gangs of murderous misogynistic boys, in which executions and atrocities are the pornographic spectacles that feed the public's hunger for sensation. No music, no literature, no art, no kite-flying, chess, movies, or photographs (except for the frequently homoerotic "official ID photos" of Taleban fighters, like those collected by Edward Grazda, hand-tinted shots of men and boys, often wearing makeup and frequently posed in amorous pairs). Everyday life as almost all human beings know it is of little or no consequence.

Five sixths of the world are infidels, unbelievers who must someday convert or die (or sometimes both: there is a long history in radical Islam of turning on recent converts, accusing them of being "Crypto-Jews" or agents sent to destabilize Islam). Nearly 20 percent of all Moslems are Shi'as, considered apostates, even worse than infidels in the eyes of Salafis: murdering Shi'a men, women, and children is considered absolutely proper in Salafi eyes: at the time of this writing, Pakistani Taleban have been sorting out Pakistani Army prisoners by religion, and cutting the heads off of many of the Shi'as they find, videotaping the executions for the delectation of their brethren in Saudi Arabia and elsewhere. Most other non-Salafi Moslems are also anathematized by Salafis, including the great majority of Sunnis in India and Pakistan, members of the Sufi-tinged Barelvi sect. Salafis in Pakistan have begun killing them and other moderate Sunnis as well.

A few years ago, a Pakistani journalist wrote a humorous piece called "The Last Moslem in Pakistan," in which he used exaggerated Salafi-type arguments to prove that one Moslem sect after another was heretical, finally declaring that the Salafis themselves were heretics, and only he was a true Moslem. It was funny, but also not far from reality.

This pathological intolerance has led Salafis to carry out acts of inconceivable cruelty and violence all over the world; when you are trying to scourge a corrupt planet of what you regard as filth, deviltry, and folly, who cares about "innocent bystanders," "collateral damage," "noncombatants," and other niceties?

It would take an encyclopedia compiled by Ambrose Bierce, the Marquis de Sade, and Heydrich the Hangman to contain the recent crimes committed by Salafis, but here are just a few, chosen for their geographic range and variety:

In the 1990s, in Pakistan, Saudi-funded Salafist groups aligned with ISI began a deliberate program of liquidating Shi'a physicians, even though these doctors treated patients regardless of which sect of Islam they belonged to.

In one case, an assassin posing as an accident victim staggered into a Shi'a-run clinic; when a doctor rushed to help him, the man stabbed him to death and escaped. In another case, a female Shi'a physician was raped and then murdered by another supposed patient. Over the years as many as two to four hundred Shi'a doctors were killed, in a country with a desperate need for trained medical workers.

The victims also include the human cannon fodder recruited by Salafi "holy men." In southern Thailand, in 2004, in the Moslem village of Suso, nineteen members of the local soccer team, aged seventeen to thirty-four, were killed when they attacked a local Thai army post armed only with knives; the soldiers were equipped with M-16 assault rifles. The villagers had been given dust blessed by a local Salafi cleric, who told them it would protect them and deter pursuers if they sprinkled it in the road behind them as they escaped. Buddhist-Moslem relations in the south of Thailand had been mostly peaceful for decades, until Wahhabi missionaries paid by Saudi "religious charities" began showing up in the 1990s, opening Salafist madrassas and mosques. Shortly thereafter, Moslem converts began kinds of attacks never seen before in the region, beheading Buddhist monks desecrating temples and bombing street markets crowded with innocent civilians.

In the fall of 2007, in eastern Afghanistan, a fourteen-year-old homeless orphan boy was caught near the provincial governor's home wearing a suicide bomber's vest. He didn't try to resist or escape;

instead, he cheerfully told the police that he was on his way to try and see the governor; a "nice man" had given him the garment, telling him that when he pressed a button it would send a burst of airborne flowers over the governor, as a sign of affection from the local people.

Raheem had told me how, on his way to Pakistan from Kabul, he had seen a peasant woman in a field, nursing a baby, screened by a grove of poplars; she was at least a hundred feet from the road, and you couldn't tell what she was doing unless you looked very, very hard. Her face was cloaked by a headscarf, and she was swaddled head to toe in heavy clothing. It was one of those blazing summer days, the hard stony fields wobbling in the heat. As he passed by, he smiled to himself, at this sign of new life, and love, amongst all the dead ends and deaths of his poor country: somehow, the Afghan people would endure; they always had.

A group of young Taleban teenagers carrying AK-47s, came down the road toward Raheem. One of them spied the woman and cried out in something between anger, outrage, and predatory joy. The woman quickly turned her back, and stepped back deeper into the shadows, but it was too late. With excited shouts, the Talebs raced across the field toward her; he told himself, not really believing it, that perhaps the Talebs would only warn the woman about her outrage against decency, slap her, and be on their way. He thought of trying to interfere, but knew it would do no good. Others were passing by, too—an old, white-bearded man, a young boy on a donkey—and he saw in their eyes what he knew they saw in his: shame, sorrow, anger—and, worst of all, *resignation*. That last feeling coiled in his belly and then tightened into a knot, a knot that felt like it was strangling the very life out of him. He couldn't breathe; he couldn't look; he couldn't hear. He couldn't look, but he did.

A terrified scream from the woman; they dragged her out into the sunlight, tearing the clothing from her torso in the process. Was it ironic—if that was what they had really wanted anyway?—to gaze upon what they loathed so much? He thought suddenly of a vile saying of one the Khyber Pushtu tribess, the much-hated Mahsud tribe: "Women have no noses, they will even eat shit."

Raheem, from sophisticated Kabul, black sheep of an old, cultured family, had never understood how a man could despise his own mother, sister, wife, daughter. Wild thoughts ran through his mind: my country has gone crazy; the worst are kings and the best are beggars, and the kings kiss the feet of perfumed Arabs and soft-bodied Pakistani mullahs. "Never trust a fat, rich mullah," the old saying went, and now it seemed that every mullah he saw in Kabul was fat, and rich, with the eyes of Iblis and as godless as a goat . . . which made him think of a jape his taxi driver friend Syed, who hated Arabs, Wahhabis, Talebs, the whole lot, had come up with: the Salafis were obsessed with beards as a sign of piety, the longer the beard the better the Moslem, and Syed said that if that were true he had seen goats with much longer beards than Osama bin Laden or Mullah Omar, and they should all pray toward the slaughterhouses where the goats' heads were hung . . .

The baby fell to the ground. They forced the woman to kneel. A volley of shots from behind—five—each as distinct as a separate death, and she fell sprawling, lifeless, the back of her head and her neck and upper body nearly obliterated. The boys (for that is what they really were) came bounding back toward the road, yelling and laughing exultantly, like a team that has just scored the winning goal. As Raheem spurred his horse and rode away, he could hear the baby, lying there in the hot stones, in the deadly sun, wailing for its mother.

• • •

But getting back to my winter tour of Talebanland:

The worst place I saw in Kabul was the city's central orphanage; here was the perfect paradigm example of the Salafi attitude toward innocence, joy, and the future of the Afghan people, and humanity as a whole.

It was located in an abandoned factory, a gutted two-story concrete building set in a vacant lot full of trash, rubbish, and scrap. Little boys in rags squatted in the dust outside, playing cheerless games with pebbles and shards of shrapnel. Inside, scores of apathetic children lay on bare bunks in gray-walled dormitory rooms. Most of the windows were broken, and it was as cold as an ice cave; God knows what it was like at night, when temperatures dropped to far below freezing; presumably the Taleban minders brought in blankets, or iron salamander heaters. My interpreter told me that the girls over ten or eleven years of age were only allowed outside for an hour each day, when they were herded up onto the rooftop; in the Taleban's twisted consciousness they were approaching puberty, and were already receptacles of shame and sin to be sequestered from the eyes of men.

There was one island of comfort, even luxury, in this institutional hell: the office where the mullahs in charge and their cronies hung out: a wood-fired stove made the room cozy, and the usual catamites served tea, cookies, and sweets. As always, the mullahs were well fed, extremely so; their bellies strained the midriffs of their soft woolen *shalwar kameezes*. At least they were friendly, unlike so many of their brethren: they urged me to drink more tea, eat another sugar cookie, move closer to the stove. Perhaps they thought they could cajole me into writing a favorable news story on their abattoir where childhoods were slaughtered.

Actually, they needn't have worried; while my reports on the war against the Russians had run in *Time*, *The New York Times Magazine*, and a half-dozen other prominent periodicals; my video from that same era had run on CBS; and my audio reporting on NPR, none of my stories on the Taleban over the next two or three years ever ran anywhere. Times had changed: the Cold War was virtually over, it was the feel-good Clinton boomtown era now, and ideology was passé: cold cash was king. U.S. oil companies were courting the Taleban to get a lucrative trans-Afghanistan pipeline deal, and Taleb mullahs with blood on their hands were being honored at George W. Bush's governor's mansion in Austin, the U.S. Capitol, and the Clinton White House; dead or suffering Afghans were now sneer fodder for the oh-so-hip, oh-so-heartless, and oh-so-irresponsible gentlemen and ladies of the American media, who once wrote and voice-overed so passionately about the Afghans' Struggle for Liberty and Rugged Individualism. More on this later.

Toward the end of my trip, my interpreter and I caught a ride with a madcap Kabuli cab driver to the front lines north of the capital, where the eastern turnoff led to the Panjshir Valley stronghold of Commander Massood and his indefatigable Tajiks and the western one dead-ended in the Bamiyan Valley stronghold of the Hazara tribe, persecuted cruelly by the Taleban and the Wahhabi Arabs because of their Shi'a faith. Another vignette of inhumanity: the machinegunner on a Taleban tank offered to demonstrate his weapon by firing on a group of Tajik schoolchildren across the river and was visibly disappointed when I declined the offer, and goon squads of teenagers whiled away the time truncheoning northbound travelers and shaking them down for small change.

There was one delightfully traditional Afghan occurence, totally unexpected: a wiry young Sufi malang stepped out into the road, enthusiastically munching on a plate glass window from one of the wrecked houses nearby, varying his diet by swallowing whole an occasional tennis ball–sized pebble or 14.5 millimeter machine-gun bullet. The whole time he breathed in and out rapidly, repeatedly reciting an incantation in Arabic.

As noted before, the Talebs disliked Sufis—they and their foreign Wahhabi friends had even taken to destroying and desecrating popular shrines and saints' tombs (*ziarats*)—but the old ways were still a powerful force among the same Pushtun villagers who made up most of Taleban's volunteer fighters.

Just as the Talebs in University Town had quailed when confronted by Raheem's *baraka*, his spiritual *essence*, the glass-, stone-, and metal-devouring holy tramp had the Taleban hoodlums totally baffled; they weren't sure what to do. They sneered, they scowled, they brandished their rubber hoses and Kalashnikovs, all to no avail: the Sufi regarded them with a faintly amused expression on his face, as if they were some kind of interesting but not very important phenomenon, like a three-legged goat or a bird flying backwards. Finally the Talebs outright commanded him to move along, clicking off the safeties on their Kalashnikovs, and he shrugged, laughed, turned on his heel, and sauntered away, still munching away on a corner of the window.

There was a funny sort of punch line postscript to all this. I had videotaped the whole scene from start to finish, with the thought that I might use it some day in a documentary on Afghan Sufis; my footage has never seen the light of day beyond my office, but after I returned to the States I kept seeing the omnivorous Sufi in the background of TV news footage of Afghanistan. He seemed to turn up wherever there was a camera running, always doing the same thing: dining on impossible objects, shrapnel, rocks, the odd bits of bombed-out building, with the Taleban standing around, fuming impotently. It was like an unspoken message from the real Afghanistan: these fools have the guns but I have the power, and guess who will still be here when the war is over and the smoke clears, eating the door handles off Mullah Omar's customized air-conditioned Pajero and washing it down with thirty-weight oil?

There are still many such mystics, holy men, in Afghanistan; most Afghans, even those with Western educations, still believe on some level in treasures guarded by djinns, vampire-like female afreets with backwards feet, and shrines with the power to grant wishes. All the Wahhabis, Salafis, Talebs, and Deobandis in the world have not shaken that ancient mythopoetic universe. In one particularly ironic case, a group of al-Qaeda Arab fighters were fleeing toward Pakistan after 9/11 when they were killed in an American airstrike. Neighboring villagers soon began spreading miraculous tales about the dead jihadis: their corpses radiated a supernatural light and emanated a sweet incense-like odor. The villagers erected a shrine over their graves, and soon tales began to spread that barren women who prayed there were becoming pregnant, and disembodied lights were seen there on dark nights. The Sufi-hating dead Salafis had been incorporated into the separate reality of Afghanistan whether they liked it or not. No wonder some old Central Asian hands called Afghanistan "the Tibet of Islam": it was a land where the old magic, secrets forgotten long, long ago in the rest of the world, still survived and overpowered other people's realities.

CHAPTER 6

DO YOU REMEMBER WHERE YOU WERE WHEN YOUR EMPIRE FELL?

I caught a UN flight from Kabul north to Mazar-i-Sharif, on the other side of the battle lines. The Northern Alliance's Uzbeks, Tajiks, and Hazaras continued to hold on to the Panjshir and Bamiyan valleys and almost everything north of the Hindu Kush range. Mazar, Afghanistan's second or third largest city, had escaped the *muj*-on-*muj* fighting that had destroyed Kabul, and it was flourishing. Hundreds of pilgrims, mostly Shi'as, visited the great Blue Mosque in the center of town daily, a vast shimmering sea-green and sky-blue edifice that required a whole tile factory of its own to replace tilework worn out by time and weather. Legend said that a dark or multihued pigeon that flew there from elsewhere turned pure white by morning. Women in skirts, shawls, high heels, and dark glasses shopped in the bazaars, computer schools were springing up everywhere, and the medical school at Mazar-i-Sharif University had just turned out another graduating class of M.D. interns, men and women.

But there was also a feeling of dread, of terrible foreboding, in the air. I visited a refugee camp full of educated women and girls from Kabul whose husbands and fathers were dead; they had fled either because they or their relatives had had jobs with the old Marxist regime—not with the secret police or propaganda ministries, but as educators, medical workers, and such—or simply because they were educated, Westernized, politically aware. That automatically put them on Taleban's hit list, for execution, imprisonment, or torture; in many cases girls as young as eleven or twelve were "given" as "wives" to Salafi fighters from Saudi Arabia, North Africa, Uzbekistan.

Somewhere I have the brief video interviews I did with several of these slender, willowy women and their daughters. Most spoke perfect English; in quiet, anxious voices, they asked me—begged me—to try to find a way to get them out of Afghanistan before Taleban continued to force their way north and captured Mazar-i-Sharif; there was no doubt in their minds, or mine, what would happen to them then.

This was one of the first of many, too many, times I was to be confronted by my powerlessness. For years I had watched defenseless Afghan villages be destroyed with total impunity by Soviet jets and helicopter gunships, watched families fleeing into the mountains clutching a few pathetic belongings, met their eyes that always asked the same, hopeless question: *Can't you help us? Can't you save us? Can't you take us away from here . . . or make those demonic machines fall from the sky, or just go away?* I can't count the hours spent cursing myself for not being a better writer, a better cameraman, someone who could tell their story properly, touch enough hearts and minds to somehow save them. Long after, I still saw their faces, heard their voices, and I despised myself for failing them. Useless scribbler; clumsy scribe. There are worse things than dying in a war; try surviving while others died all around you, *because you just weren't good enough at your craft.*

Young men think that war is where you go to prove yourself, and if you don't break, if you behave courageously enough, you will be rewarded with pride, glory, and a kind of joy that will last you the rest of your life. Well, I no longer believe that: win or lose, war rewards you the same, with disillusion, desolation, sorrow, and shame. And you don't find that out until it is too late. A friend of mine, a British correspondent, had the following passage written in his notebook: "A man who hasn't been to war isn't worth a damn; he doesn't know anything, about how precious a good life is, and how obscene an untimely death is; how wonderfully brave and selfless man can be, and how incredibly evil and ugly; how absolutely insane war is, and how often it is absolutely necessary to put a stop to something even worse. If you've never been to war, you never know anything of that; but having been there, you'll wish you had never gone. Those same truths ensure that you will never really laugh or smile again, not the way you did before: that will be your reward."

In May 1997, a few months after my visit, the Taleban succeeded in occupying Mazar-i-Sharif and much of northern Afghanistan, aided by a rebel Uzbek commander, Malik Pahlawan. They only held the city for two weeks before they were driven out by an alliance of Hazaras, Massood's Tajiks, and Uzbeks loyal to Dostam; they would not return until the summer of 1998, when they forced Dostam into exile; Mazar-i-Sharif would remain a Taleban stronghold until Dostam recaptured the city with the help of U.S. air power in the aftermath of 9/11. But it was all too late for the Kabuli women and girls in the refugee camps; according to everything I have been able to find out, they were killed during the first hours of the first Taleban occupation, in 1997. I am not sure I want to know any of the details concerning how they died.

Anyone who has read Khaled Hosseini's fine novel *The Kite Runner* has a pretty good idea of how the Hazara tribe suffered under Taleban, and even before that. As Shi'a Moslems in a predominantly Sunni country, and ethnic Sino-Tibetans (they are decendants of Genghis Khan's invading Mongols and earlier immigrants from the east) amid tribes of Indo-European origin, they have always been Afghanistan's designated victims. As late as the early twentieth century, the Pushtun rulers in Kabul regularly raided the Hazara heartland in and around the Bamiyan Valley taking slaves, killing tens of thousands of civilians at a time, and building pyramids of skulls in celebration. The prejudice even shows up in contemporary Afghan censuses; Hazaras are regularly undercounted, by tens or hundreds of thousands, further weakening their already minimal political influence in the country.

Pushed back into the highest, driest, most barren parts of Afghanistan's interior, or driven into exile in the slums of Kabul and other Afghan cities and towns, as far afield as Iran, the Hazara people have somehow survived through dogged persistence and an innate genius for adaptability, born of direst necessity. During the Raj, thousands of Hazaras left their homeland to work in coal mines in present-day India; during the First World War, many of them enlisted in the British Indian Army and served as sappers on the Western Front, tunneling under the German lines to set off huge explosive devices and defending against similar attacks by the enemy. Today, thousands of Hazaras work in the oil fields of Iran and at any other jobs Iranians won't take because they are too dirty, dangerous, and poorly paid.

When I first came to Afghanistan in 1972, traveling overland from Europe, the first Afghans I really got to know were the Hazaras who worked at the Sharkh Hotel, the classic low-budget hippie/ruck-sackers' stopover in the border city of Herat. Paid pennies a day, sleeping in glorified dustbins in closets and stairwells, dressed in rags and patches, the Hazara kids at the hotel spent every spare second chatting up the guests: not for money, help with a visa, or any of the usual motives Third World people have for cultivating tourists and travelers; it was more like they were cramming for some imaginary academic entrance exam, and we *farranji* had all the answers.

First, they wanted to learn as many languages as possible: one room service waiter, who couldn't have been a day over fourteen, already spoke good English, German, French, Japanese, Hindi, Urdu, and smatterings of Spanish, Dutch, and Swedish, in addition to Pushtu, Dari, and Hazragi, his native tongue. After that, they were hungry for facts about the world beyond Afghanistan: how many people lived in New York, London, America, India? Were Communists really all atheists? Was the Christian God the same as Allah? How long would it take to walk from Kabul to Paris? To fly? How wide was the ocean, and how deep? Did Americans and Europeans really eat the flesh of pigs? Was it true that Western women could have more than one husband? Who were better: Moslems, Iranians, Arabs, or Afghans? Could a Moslem own a business in America? A car? Two cars? A house?

What did Americans think of Afghanistan? What did *I* think? Would I let my daughter marry an Afghan? A Hazara? Did I think Jesus was a man, or a God? Why did I travel to Afghanistan? Who paid for my ticket? Was the government of America good? Who was stronger, India or Pakistan? (Correct answer: "Afghanistan could beat both of them in a war.") Do the police in your country arrest innocent people?

They were full of dreams, inchoate visions of a better future, a stubborn kind of pride, and faith that their lives could be better— could be *made* better, by hard work, the acquisition of knowledge and skill, and a little help from God and his prophets and saints, who they believed were put on earth to help the poor and down-trodden: Liberation Theology in a turban. In the minds of Shi'as, paradise on earth lies not in the past, in the lives of the Prophet and his contemporaries. Mohammed delivered Allah's blueprints for a just and righteous society, but his vision was hijacked by kings and their corrupt allies in the clergy, and finally destroyed at Karbala, on October 8, AD 630, the day called Ashura, when the ancestors of today's Shi'a failed to fight on the side of Mohammed's grandson Hussein and his followers, who were trying to preserve the vision. To the Hazaras and other Shi'as, this was the great cosmic tragedy, not only for them but for all of humanity. "All days are Ashura, all lands are Karbala," as the famous Shi'a apothegm puts it: the E = mc², the crucifixion of Shi'ism, in which a small, one-sided battle, a 40,000-member Sunni army against less than 150 Believers, in a dusty corner of the Tigris-Euphrates valley, becomes the ageless rallying point for good against evil.[3]

Early in the winter of 1997, I got a phone call at my house in the Colorado rockies from an old friend, a doctor whom I had worked with in Afghanistan before. He had been asked by a rather eccentric little aid group to lead a medical team to Bamiyan, at the invitation

---

[3] It also makes mush of Samuel Huntington's tragically skewed historical model, that the "War on Terror" is part of a "Clash of Civilizations" between an enlightened, rational, tolerant West and a reactionary, bigoted, and homicidal Islam. All three monotheistic faiths—Judaism, Christianity, and Islam—contain their quotient of "holy warriors": West Bank settlers and advocates of ethnically cleansing Palestine; "Mosque-Buster"/ "I Stepped in Some Shi'ite"/"Kick His Ass and Take His Gas" Christians; suicide bombing, Holocaust-denying Moslems ... They all resemble each other far, far more than they do their decent, big-hearted coreligionists.

of the Hizb-i-Wahdat, the Hazara tribe's political/military wing. The team, which had over half a ton of medical supplies with them, was taking off from Los Angeles in two or three days, and if I made it there in time there was a ticket waiting for me, roundtrip LAX-Seoul-Bangkok-Tashkent (the capital of Uzbekistan) and on to Termez, which is on the Uzbekistan-Pakistan border just north of Mazar-i-Sharif.

From Termez, the Hazaras would fly us in their last patched-up Antonov twin-engined transport (they had once had twenty; the other nineteen had either crashed or been shot down. The team really needed me, my friend said, to liaison with the local Afghans, and hopefully to cover the mission and generate some publicity for the Hazara cause: they were now surrounded on all four sides by Taleban, with enemy forces just over Shebar Pass to the east, and steadily inching their way north through the Koh-i-Baba mountains, south of Bamiyan; their main link to the outside world, Mazar-i-Sharif, had already been occupied once by Taleban and was being threateed again; and there was a famine throughout the Hazara territory, with whole villages starving to death. The airstrip at Bamiyan had been repeatedly bombed, so badly cratered it was unusable; United Nations and other aid personnel either helicoptered in or used the remote runway at Shebertoo.

But the point was, the Hazaras really needed us, or believed they did; and who could say no and ever look at themselves in the mirror again?

I had been regularly commuting from Colorado to L.A., where I had been getting odd jobs as a screenwriter, and I had the trip nailed at less than fifteen hours, nonstop and averaging seventy-five in my old Ford Explorer. Running late as usual, I headed out at dawn, seventeen hours before departure time out of LAX. The first omens were ill ones: it was barely past six, my gas tank showed near empty, and the Conoco didn't open 'til seven. I turned around and drove home, and sat there fidgeting away the minutes, watching the clock 'til 6:55. Then Lizard Head Pass was unexpectedly stormy, slow going, with axle-deep slush and periods of spindrift and whiteout when I couldn't see past the hood. There were minefields of black ice on the swooping curves beyond Rico, and then a long succession of terrified tourists, flatlanders, crawling along at thirty miles per hour or less and then inexplicably speeding up whenever I tried to pass. I was two hours down when, as I entered Cortez, Colorado, the Ford's muffler broke loose without warning. I crept through town making a godawful racket, scraping up a trail of sparks in my wake. The local muffler shop said they could weld the muffler back on in an hour, just as soon as the welder made it in—sometime that morning. It would cost me a hundred dollars. I counted the bankroll in my pocket: twelve twenty dollar bills. Figuring in gas, I should still have close to a hundred when, *if,* I finally flew out of L.A. Done.

By the time I left Cortez (the welding took less than an hour, but waiting for the welder to show proved to be a Samuel Beckett three-act-er—household chores and a dog that had to go to the vet) the day was approaching the waning point. It was clear that I wouldn't make it on time via road; in fact, it wasn't clear that I would make it at all, unless one of my Sufi friends from Afghanistan showed up with a magic carpet. I half-considered turning around and going home, but the shame would have been almost palpable. I thought of alternatives, and when I got to Flagstaff in the late afternoon I just kept going, south toward Phoenix instead of peeling off on I-40, the usual Needles to Barstow run.

It was dark when I got to the airport in Phoenix, and unless the flight to Bangkok was delayed I would never make it; I had just about an hour, max. I found a spot in the closest parking lot, grabbed my duffel bag, and caught a shuttle to the terminal, and as I sprinted toward the ticket counter I caught sight of the local time on a digital clock in a newsstand: it was *six oh three*, not *seven oh three: idiot!* Unbelievably, I had totally forgotten the time change, from Rocky Mountain to Pacific Coast. I was just in time to pay cash for the next LAX flight, leaving in twenty minutes.

I was dropping money, I.D, car keys everywhere; an awful way to begin a trip halfway around the world, to a war zone.

The flight to Los Angeles actually landed on time, and I bull-rushed the aisle, aided by a flight attendant whom I had informed about my impending connecting flight and the reason my journey—"medical aid—team of doctors—famine and war." A quick look at the DEPARTURE screens in the terminal, a thousand-meter obstacle course run, and I arrived at the United Bangkok flight whatever economy check-in line just in time to see my doctor friend and two companions about to get their boarding passes, the doc anxiously scanning the crowded terminal while the ticket agent looked over his passport. As his gaze turned my way I waved my arms in the air; he focused, squinted, and then broke into a huge smile. A moment later I had been moved up the line to join my three fellow team members, and then we were all shaking hands and talking and laughing at the same time; there was much amusement as I recounted the day's events. I caught a glimpse of my reflection in the window of a coffee shop on the way to the gate: my knees were covered with dried mud, from my fruitless crawling attempts to re-anchor the muffler with gaffer tape; my ski cap was a sodden, shapeless mass, more accident than hat; I was soaked, with snowmelt and flop sweat, and the zipper on my duffel had broken, threatening to spill the contents everywhere. Still, I was on my way . . .

That first Bamiyan trip really marked the beginnig of my serious involvement with Salafism, al-Qaeda and particular. It was a crazed journey start to finish—Colorado to Bamiyan and back in ten days, in winter and wartime—but that only seemed to make the issues that much more intense.

The trip as far as Tashkent was virtually nonstop: a few hours on the ground in both Seoul and Bangkok, then onward. There was a disquieting interlude on the Bangkok-Tashkent flight, when we encountered a couple of junior Foreign Service officers and their wives, returning to the embassy in Tashkent after a week or so of R & R, stocking up on booze, groceries, DVDs, videos, books, and magazines.

The docs tried to winkle some beta on the Uzbekistan situation out of them—"Stake a fellow American to some inside-story intel, brother?"—but when we told them where we were ultimately headed, they instantly chilled up: "Do you know what kind of trouble you could cause the government of the United States? The Hazaras are Shi'as, you know. Do you want to end up being snatched by the Revolutionary Guard's Al Quds brigade and waking up in an Iranian prison, sentenced to hang for spying? I can't tell you not to go, but if anything happens to you, you're on your own—don't expect us to come riding to the rescue," etc., etc., ad infinitum.

Schmucks.

In Tashkent we were chauffered around by the local security police. They all wore the same black leather jackets and carried cell phones that they used constantly to check in with "headquarters"; occasionally you glimpsed a Makarov 9mm automatic discretely tucked away in a shoulder holster; they drove slick shiny black SUV sedans. Despite their "secret police" status, they were very friendly; almost all of them were ethnic Hazaras whose families had emigrated north from Afghanistan decades ago, and they were obviously pleased that we were going to try and help their fellow Hazaras fight against the Taleban and Wahhabi Arabs.

The leg down to Termez, the border town on the north bank of the Amu Darya river, was on another Uzbek Air flight. Bangkok to Tashkent the airline flew 757s, with British and Aussie pilots; the flight to Termez was something out of the old Soviet Union, an antedated cigar-shaped Ilyushin with an Uzbek crew and dilapidated seats. As we boarded, I glanced down and noticed that one of the plane's six tires was totally, 100 percent flat. It not only wasn't a no smoking flight, it was very nearly *all smoking*; before we even moved out from the gate 90 percent of the passengers were puffing away on cheap Russian cigarettes and passing around plastic screw-top bottles of execrable lukewarm Bulgarian vodka. When we accelerated toward takeoff, the flat tire emitted an off-kilter drumming sound, like a jalopy with wheels out of alignment and a tie rod about to go.

At the Termez airport, you felt like you were on the edge of a war zone. KGB Border Guards in their distinctive blue and white striped T-shirts and bulky parachutists' smocks hung around everywhere, looking like professional soldiers: some mean and sneering, some bored to death, some looking like they just fell off a hay truck on their way to junior high school. They all carried those lethal little folding-stock AKMSes, the kind favored by elite Russian troops, helicopter pilots and bodyguards.

I recognized a raffish figure in a bright red shirt, a wide white tie and an awful brown double-breasted pin-striped suit, with greasy pompadoured hair; it was the Ismaili warlord—his name eluded me—from Pol-i-Khumri, just north of the Salang Tunne, who had led a brutal pro-Soviet militia during the '80s and '90s. Ismailis are a sub-sect of Shi'ism—the Agha Khan is probably its most famous adherent—and when Taleban captured Pol-i-Khumri he and his top cronies wisely hoofed it north. One of them was with him now, an enormously fat man, unshaven, who looked like the lost twin brother of Sergeant Garcia, the comic-relief villain on the ancient Disney TV series, *Zorro*. The two were on their way to a United Nations-brokered peace conference somewhere in Europe, to be attended by Taleban, their Pakistani backers, neighboring countries like Iran, Tajikistan and Uzbekistan, and representatives of different anti-Taleban political and ethnic groups ranging from the Northern Alliance and the former head of Jamiat-i-Islami Professor Rabbani to glorified mafiosas like the Pol-i-Khumri "government" in exile. Poor, poor Afghanistan.

The warlord had actually been head of an outlaw motorcycle gang and a part-time pizza delivery man in Pennsylvania when the Sovs invaded Afghanistan in '79; he returned home not out of patriotism, but because his instincts told him there was easy money to be made off the Jihad. Upon arriving, he recruited a makeshift militia from among his fellow-Ismailis, and rented them out to the Russians as security guards on the main north-souh highway from Kabul to Uzbekistan and Tajikistan. In addition, he traded in stolen weapons, gems and drugs; he and his Soviet army officer friends were one of the major links in the flow of Afghan opium and heroin to the booming population of addicts in the former Soviet Union and Eastern Europe.

A journalist I know once celebrated Christmas at the warlord's palatial villa in Pol-i-Khumri. The warlord had a giant model train system set up around his house, running through every room; on Christmas morning a train came chugging into the guest bedroom where my friend was sleeping and came to a stop. The whistle hooted, and my friend opened his eyes to see an open hopper car next to his pillow: in it was a plastic baggie of heroin, a loaded syringe, and a card with a laughing Santa Claus on the front; the message inside said, "Season's Greetings from a Dear Friend."

The next morning, we took off for the temporary Independent State of Hazaristan. It was a daunting departure. The plane looked like it was held together with welded and bolted patches; there was no insignia or numbering anywhere on the fuselage, only a faded Afghan Air Force roundel from the era of the old Marxist regime in Kabul, the air force of a regime that no longer existed. Ghost flight: if it went down no one would ever look for it, and if it made the news it would be in the form of a tiny item buried in the back pages, along with stories like "Turkish Train Strike Averted" and "Floods Kill 93 in Coomaraswamy." The boxes of medical supplies were stacked haphazardly down the center of the cabin; we sat in fold-down seats, facing inward.

It was one of those moments when you have to imagine yourself later in the flight—with a Taleban MiG closing in on the lumbering prop plane out of a crystal-clear sky, the sharp-toothed mountains of the Paropamisus two thousand, three thousand feet below, no escape—wishing you'd had the nerve to jump up before the plane started rolling and yell, "Sorry, I'm not going!" And then, at the last second, the door reopens, and a smiling, Hazara enters and begins handing out fresh pomegranates to everybody on board, a parting present, and the temperature in your heart instantly plummets to below freezing . . .

Before you ever went into Afghanistan, into the war, you had a strange, strange dream, unlike any you had ever had before or since. The gods were weighing your soul, and finding it wanting: the only way to redeem yourself was to go back to Afghanistan and try to help those people you had loved so much when you were there in peacetime, in the '70s . . . especially the Sufi peddler you met in Herat, and sat with in the bazaar day after day, a wordless teacher who communicated solely by smiling, and gazing into your eyes . . .

In the dream I told the gods I was frightened of going to war, and I asked them if they could guarantee my safety there; they laughed and laughed, and shook their heads: "*But that would be cheating*," they said, and I couldn't help laughing along with them. Then the dream shifted: I was in a cave in Afghanistan, and a basket of pomegranates appeared before me, and somehow I knew that the fruit that marked the doorway between life and death . . . it was not meant for the living.

Later you researched it, and it turned out pomegranates were exactly that, according to ancient lore: what you ate as you stood on the threshold of eternal darkness, as you prepared to step off . . . "Watch that next step, it's a big one. Back on the airplane I stared at the basket of fruit and shook my head, unable to speak, paralyzed. I tensed my muscle, preparing to rise and follow the gift-bearer out the door.

But then you look over at your friends' faces, and they are all drawn, bloodless, attempting to smile back at you with twitching lips, except for the doc, who was an old soldier pushing retirement age back when the Greeks defeated the Persians at Samothrace, for Zeus's sake . . . He gives you a wink and a thumbs-up. And the three or four Hazara passengers on board are smiling encouragingly, so happy that you, someone, *anyone*, has cared enough to travel all the way here on their behalf, when it seemed that the rest of the world couldn't care less if they lived or died. . . . The Pomegranate Man leaps from the plane, the door slams shut, the engines throttle up to a deafening roar; we pivot, taxi a few feet, and suddenly we are bumping down the runway, banging through potholes . . . we leap from the tarmac, and for better or for worse we are bound for the Great Unknown.

There were no windows in the plane. A few minutes after takeoff the pilot called back from the cockpit, and one of the Hazara passengers translated: "We've crossed over. Into Afghanistan air."

This is how you get killed, I said to myself. Wars were full of moments like this, decisions where you weighed the odds over and over again, tweaked your instincts and senses to try and pick up any stray vibe or unlikely factor that might mean survival or the opposite. In the end, you had to trust in luck. No one is more superstitious than soldiers and war correspondents; all too often they've seen some preternaturally skilled comrade zapped while

Gomer Pyle, Beetle Bailey, Doberman, or Good Soldier Švejk
blundered on unscathed. Lucky or death-defying funny tat-
toos (*If Balls Missing Do Not Resuscitate*), amulets (a tiger tooth;
a quartz crystal; a bald or golden eagle feather; a page from the
Koran rolled up tight in a silver cylinder; the AK-47 slug that was
headed straight for your spinal column but lodged in your ALICE
pack instead, slowed and finally stopped by copies of Field Manual
44-18-1 and F.M. ST 31-918, two MRES, a knotted-up British
SAS *shemagh*, and, most important, a spare SAPI plate), rituals and
taboos ("Never talk about miraculous escapes—the times you were
almost killed but somehow escaped; you don't want to remind the
spirits that you're still around"), graffiti on helmets and vehicles,
etc., etc.

You learn a lot about people by getting to know their enemies; so
it was with the Hazaras.

We landed at Shebertoo in the aftermath of a big blizzard that
had dumped five or six feet of snow across the mountains. The local
Hizb-i-Wahdat garrison, gawky high school age kids in baggy war
surplus fatigues and hats with huge earflaps, had hand-shoveled the
whole runway down to the bare ground. As we exited the plane,
they cheered enthusiastically, and a group of older men, officials and
mullahs, surrounded us, wringing our hands and salaaming. I found
myself thinking of those U.S. diplomats on the Bangkok-Tashkent
flight, and their wild warnings: were they misinformed, ignorant, or
was something much, much more nastier going on?

It was a long, long road, from Shebertoo down to Bamiyan, and every head-high frozen mile of it had been cleared by hand and shovel by villagers along the way; even then it was a hazardous journey, the battered Chinese-made military trucks sliding sideways down slopes of mud and ice, threatening to tip over and roll, grinding low gears as we slithered down breakneck gullies.

Every few miles there was a clump of adobe-walled buildings, and a mob of people, men, women, and children, cheering, holding up painted signs: WELCOME OUR AMERICAN FRIENDS, THANK YOU FROM THE HAZARA PEOPLE, BAMIYAN WELCOMES YOUR HELP. Tiny schoolchildren half-sang, half-shouted, determined that their greetings be heard. You could see how poor the Hazaras were: barren treeless hills rose to serried snow peaks, mountains without names.

As we approached Bamiyan, sentinels began to appear on every wall hilltop and crag, lone figures with AK-47s, RPG-7s, or Enfields, guardians watching over the ancient core of the Hazara Nation. Cliffs closed in on the left, sandstone perforated with caves and holes, many of which had wooden ladders leading up to them, and grey smoke from cooking fires coiling up into the chill air. Whole families of Hazara refugees, survivors of ethnic cleansing in the rest of Afghanistan, were wintering there.

The center of the town, the bazaar and the government buildings, was a gutted, charred sea of rubble subdivided by grids of demolished walls, bombed out by Taleban. Bamiyan dated back to the Silk Road and before, one of the tenuous string of oases—water, pasture, and shelter—that linked Venice with Beijng, and on to Japan. Silk, Buddha, gunpowder, pasta, Greek art, Nestorian Christianity, Judaism, and Islam, the lotus, zero, the self-supporting arch, baths, fractal numbers, the stirrup, the tempered steel sword, tea and the porcelain cup to drink it from . . . all these and ten times more traveled east to west or west to east twenty centuries or more ago, and places like Bamiyan were what made it possible.

And then, there, without warning, were the two great standing Buddhas in their adjacent niches, the first 180 feet high, the second 125; they were virtually faceless, which only added to their otherworldly aura. One of the Pushtun conquerors of the valley had sawed the top half of the face off the taller figure, while the smaller "female" one's features had almost completely eroded away; they gazed, eyeless, across the valley, beyond the surface of space and time . . .

I quickly discovered that something remarkable was happening here, or trying to happen, even as crackpots and crazies from Hell tried to reverse-engineer the rest of Afghanistan and sink it back into the Dark Ages.

The Hazaras were being threatened on all sides by the Taleban and al-Qaeda, who had already slaughtered thousands of Hazara civilians; during the fighting for Kabul, the Taleban captured Hizb-i-Wahdat's leader Mazari under a flag of truce during "peace negotiations," tortured him, and then threw him out of a helicopter over Kabul. The Hazaras really had no friends among the anti-Taleban forces, either: Massood's Tajiks had wiped out whole neighborhoods of Hazaras during the battle for Kabul, Uzbeks and Hazaras in Mazr-i-Sharif were constantly at each other's throats, and the pro-Pushtun Pakistani government discriminated against Hazara refugees attempting to cross the border to safety, rounding them up into internment camps. Even Iran, which supposedly aided the Hazaras because of their common Shi'ite religious faith, had damaged the Hazaras' cause as much as they had helped it: many of the tribe's most effective leaders during the anti-Soviet jihad had been assassinated by pro-Iranian agents more interested in Teheran's interests than in the Hazaras' welfare, and the amount of aid the Iranians managed to get through to the Hazaras was only a fraction of what was needed.

Just recently, a group of Hizb-i-Wahdat *mujahedin* had demanded the removal of the large portrait of Ayatollah Khomeini on the outer wall of the Iranian Consulate in Bamiyan—"We don't need Khomeini, we have our own leaders," they said—and when the Iranians refused they began attempting to erase the giant face with bullets and rocket-propelled grenades. The Iranians were now barricaded in their compoumd, under virtual siege by Hazara fighters.

Despite all this, there was a sense of hope, of excitement about the future, in Bamiyan. Many of the caves in the cliffs surrounding the Buddhas were being used as schoolrooms for girls and women; the same hunger for education I had noticed in Herat years ago was alive here, for females as well as males. Almost every mosque in the valley had its girls school, adult education classes, and a women's crafts center. Every boy and girl you talked to dreamed of being a computer programmer, doctor, teacher, pilot. Then there was Bamiyan University, a coed multiethnic institution housed in a complex of adobe buildings at the eastern edge of town; as many as four hundred students, Pushtuns, Tajiks, Uzbeks, attended classes there, in English, pre-med sciences, math, and engineering.

Hazaras in both Bamiyan and Mazar-i-Sharif were publishing magazines, on topics ranging from poetry and feminism to political philosophy—I saw one article on Thomas Paine and the democratic ideal—and striking posters celebrating the Hazaras' cultural heritage and ethnic pride. The Health Ministry of Hizb-i-Wahdat was headed by a woman doctor, and the Hazaras' militia included a corps of nurses armed with AK-47 assault rifles.

When I walked up to the base of the cliff to see the Buddhas at close range, I was accompanied by a tall, ruddy-faced mullah in turban and robes who told me about how his people had built these huge statues "before we learned the truth of the Koran." We passed signs urging visitors to RESPECT THE BUDDHAS, and a couple of kids in padded parkas and sheepskin-lined caps standing guard with Kalashnikovs. Later, in his office (the mullah was one of the leaders of Hizb-i-Wahdat), I filmed an interview with him; he proudly showed me a parchment page from a Jewish liturgical text that a farmer had unearthed in a nearby field a few months before: "Once some of us were Buddhists, then some were Jewish; now we are Shi'a.

But don't film me holding this page, or our Iranian friends might be angry," he said with a conspiratorial smile.

Several Hazaras told me they dreamed of the days when tourists came from all over the world to see the wonders of Bamiyan, which included the Cave of the Tears of the Dragon, lava fields and geysers, the ruins of Shahr-i-Gholghola, the City of Screams (destroyed by Genghis Khan's Mongols in 1221), and the turquoise-blue lakes of Band-i-Amir. There would be a museum at the feet of the Buddhas, housing the finest artifacts from the Hazaras' past, including artifacts from hundreds of sites not yet discovered, let alone excavated.

According to legend, there was a Reclining Buddha even grander than the two standing images—the longest Reclining Buddha in the world, either hidden away in a cave in a far corner of the Bamiyan Valley or buried underground—perhaps at the very feet of the two upright Buddhas. It sounded far-fetched, until you remembered that the Minaret of Jam, the tallest minaret in the world, wasn't really "discovered" until well into the twentieth century, when a DC-3 pilot, blown way off course by a Central Asian dust storm, caught a glimpse of it, stuck in the throat of a narrow gorge fifty or a hundred miles from the nearest dirt road, to the west of Bamiyan.

All of these beautiful visions and brave dreams came in the midst of a growing catastrophe that threatened the very existence of the Hazara people. They were being slaughtered by the hundreds wherever Taleban and al-Qaeda forces found them. Bamiyan Valley was filling up with refugees, camping out in abandoned farmhouses, caves, and ragged tents; with temperatures dropping far below zero every night, the snow piled up head-high, and the winds slashing like a razor, countless numbers were dying. You knew terrible things must have happened to these displaced hordes, to drive them out in the worst part of a Hindu Kush winter. Ask them about it, and they could barely bring themselves to speak; some things truly are "unspeakable." All you really had to do was look into their eyes: the whole story was there.

Even worse in terms of sheer numbers of dead was the famine that was sweeping Hazaristan, wiping out whole villages, districts. The people at the World Food Program office weren't allowed to talk about it—any kind of bad publicity and Taleban would shut down their operations throughout all of Afghanistan—but I managed to get some rough figures put together by people who had actually been out in the field. At least one hundred thousand dead, maybe as many as three hundred thousand. One hundred percent malnutrition over 90 percent of Hazaristan.

And this was only mid-winter.

Famines in the twentieth and twenty-first century are almost always man-made, a deliberate part of a military or political campaign, and this one was no exception. The Hazaras have always survived through trade. Most of their land is unfarmable, but suitable for livestock grazing; every fall, the Hazaras drove their surplus sheep and goats down out of the mountains and traded them for enough wheat, rice, cooking oil, and so on to make it through the lean winter months. The Taleban had simply put a halt to that trade, blockading all movements of foodstuff in and out of Hazaristan. Now it was having its desired effect: hundreds of thousands of Hazaras were dead or dying.

Before I left the States, I had talked with an editor at *Time* magazine about the famine story; my Hazara friends in the U.S., two of whom worked at Voice of America, as well as the Hazaras who had helped the docs organize their aid mission, had given me enough convincing evidence on the subject to interest the *Time* man. I had done a half dozen or so Afghanistan stories for the magazine, from 1984 through the early '90s; interest in the area had fallen sharply since the Soviets left and the Marxist regime in Kabul fell, but according to the editor the immense scope of the current famine, and the fact that a gigantic act of genocide was being carried out without any attention from the outside world, just might be enough to squeeze a story into the world news section. He gave me his office number, and told me to call him anytime during office hours; he would instruct his "personal assistant" to put my call through no matter what. That had been less than a week before; the next day I had flown home to Colorado, and two days after that I was making my Don Quixote-ish way to LAX via Lizard Head Pass, muffler shop, and Phoenix.

I computed the time difference between New York and Bamiyan, and late that night I put on my ski parka and boots and trudged down to the Hizb-i-Wahdat communications office, accompanied by one of our Hazara interpreters. Our footsteps squeaked in the bitterly cold, dry snow; you could see into every nook and cranny of the Milky Way, as if the night sky had been eviscerated and its radiant interior spread open, to be studied and cataloged. The two Buddhas gazed serenely into the void.

A kid in a padded parka sat in a chair by the front door, an AK-47 across his lap; he leapt to his feet as we approached. The three of us exchanged greetings, and he held the door open for us as we entered. The commo center was a single adobe-walled room, one wall covered by a seven-by-nine-foot map of Afghanistan, a mosaic of satellite images. Some of the rough-trimmed roof beams still oozed driblets of amber tangy-smelling conifer sap. The center must have been built on top of the ruins, after this part of town was bombed flat by the Taleban.

Somewhere a generator throbbed. Three or four Hazaras sat at tables, monitoring radios, talking in short, clipped phrases or listening to disembodied voices swathed in crackling static, the beeps, honks, and whistles of a message pinballing around the troposphere.

Someone brought me a cup of scalding *sheen chai*, green tea. A second person took the satellite phone—one of two at the Hizb-i-Wahdat office in Bamiyan—out of a briefcase, switched it on, and handed it to me. Someone else handed me a flashlight. I drank as much of the tea as I could without causing permanent injury to my throat, dug my single page of notes on the famine from my parka pocket, and began slowly sweeping the sky for a satellite. Walking down to the commo center, I hadn't realized just how cold it was; now, standing still, my toes were going numb, my fingers were on fire, and my ears and nose felt brittle, like you could snap them off.

The phone locked on to a satellite at last, and I punched in the country and city codes and the number of the editor's office at *Time*. I imagined how excited people would be at that end: few correspondents were being allowed into Afghanistan then, and nobody had gotten into Bamiyan to report on the Hazaras' situation.

"Hello, ——— ———'s office. Can I help you?"

"Uh, yes, hello. This is Rob Schultheis—I met with ——— ——— about the Afghanistan story last week—the famine—."

"——— ——— is in his morning meeting. You'll have to call back later—."

I could almost see the phone descending— "He told me to call him anytime during office hours, that he would take the call. See, I'm on a satellite phone, in Afghanistan, in the mountains, in the snow—it's the middle of the night here—."

An audible sigh: "I'll try and reach him."

A few seconds later I heard a muffled colloquy; it went on longer than it should have. I stamped up and down in the snow to resuscitate my feet.

The line went live again. "What did you say your name was?"

"*Rob Schultheis*. I'm reporting from *Afghanistan*—I'm there—."

But she was already gone. I heard more indecipherable dialogue. Then: "——— ——— says you'll have to call him back some other time, when he's not in a conference, Mister, ah—."

"*Schultheis*. Listen, it's really kind of hard—."

And the phone went off.

I finished my thought, into the dead phone: "—to try and call from here. I'm not at fucking Penn Station."

As I reentered the commo building, the young guard jumped up.

"*Khub?*"—Good?—indicating the phone and my call.

I made myself smile, and nod: "*Khub*—very good!" *These people deserved a lot more than I was delivering*, I told myself for the thousandth time since I first came to wartime Afghanistan; the least I could do was act encouraging.

Americans: they murder so casually, with an averted eye, an ironic remark, a yawn . . . unindicted coconspirators in how many outrages, how many crimes?

•   •   •

I had collected a number of first-person accounts of Taleban atrocities and war crimes against Hazaras, as well as evidence of the ongoing famine and its causes, but when I got back to the States the *Time* editor who had been so interested in a Hazara story didn't return my phone calls. I wrote several op-ed/news pieces datelined Bamiyan, but all were greeted by that classic "MEGO" syndrome: looking at the listeners, you just knew they were mentally compiling a list of the ten worst holes of golf they had ever played.

I struck out with every editor, magazine, and newspaper, every talk show maven or yakkety-yakking head I had ever known: what freelance journalists and stringers call "melting down the old Rolodex."

And then there was the State Department: I had the phone number of someone in the "human rights" office, courtesy of a friend, and I called her up, expecting at least a sympathetic ear; instead I got Big Brothered, big-time: "We've heard those same reports, Mister Shoo-ties, and we have no way of ascertaining if they are genuine, or just more of the propaganda that gets tossed around in situations of ethnic feuding—."

"I'd hardly call this 'feuding,' when one side is systematically slaughtering the other, who happen to be totally unarmed. I mean, doesn't somebody have to shoot back before you call it feuding? Or is this the same old story of tabooing the 'G-word'?" The Clinton Administration had become both notorious and a laughingstock for their frantic attempts to avoid using the word "genocide" during the breakup of Yugoslavia. In their tiny minds, "genocide" would mean they actually had to take action, which would have poisoned the Feel Good/Greed Is Great *Weltanschauung* Clinton and company so loved.

"Well, as I said, Mister Shoo-ties, since we don't really know what events led up to the incidents in question, like who provoked whom, the government of the United States is hardly in the position of being able to appoint itself judge, prosecutor, and jury. And as I said the last time we spoke, without material evidence or testimony by a neutral third party we don't even know if something happened, let alone who if anyone was to blame—."

I didn't put it all together at the time, but during this same general period Unocal, the West Coast–based energy giant, was courting the Taleban, hoping to get the rights for a lucrative Turkmenistan-to-Pakistan trans-Afghanistan pipeline project, and genocidal Taleban mullahs were everywhere, slithering and slything their way from Capitol Hill to the Clinton Department of State to George Doubya Bush's gubernatorial digs in Austin, Texas. Who cared about a bunch of cave-dwelling Shi'ites whose land didn't have a drop of oil under it? And then there were our old "friends," the Saudi Arabians and Pakistanis: they loved the Taleban and hated the Hazaras, which was good enough for everyone in America who counted, who had money, influence, connections. What was it Stalin said, when told the Vatican disapproved of something he did? "How many divisions does the Pope have?" Well, how many barrels of light sweet crude did the Hazaras have? Case closed.

I returned to Hazaristan the following summer, on a World Food Program flight from Peshawar; this time the airstrip at Bamiyan was open. I was hoping to get more evidence about the famine, and the WFP office in Kabul agreed to help me. As before, no one in the U.S. was interested in the Hazara story, so I was paying for the whole trip myself; maybe someone would buy some videotape when I got home, though I wasn't counting on it. As far as the outside world was concerned, Afghanistan and its sorrows no longer existed. If anyone was concerned about South Asia, they were focused on India and Pakistan: the Indians had recently detonated five "nuclear devices," atomic bombs, just before I left Pakistan, and a couple of days after I arrived in Bamiyan the Pakistanis answered by exploding five of their own.

While I was in Bamiyan, I accompanied a WFP convoy on a surreal mission across the front lines into Taleban territory. The World Food Program wanted to send an emergency shipment of wheat, 650 tons, into the southern part of Hazaristan, where the effects of the famine were still being felt. The wheat was being stored at Ghazni, in Taleban territory. The Taleban demanded that the WFP give *them* 650 tons of wheat, too, even though they didn't really need it, just to be "fair."

It just so happened that there was an isolated enclave of Taleban turf just west of Bamiyan, over Shebar Pass: the Ghorband Valley, surrounded by Hazara territory on the east and Massood's Tajiks on the other three sides. The WFP agreed to truck 650 tons of the wheat they had stockpiled in Bamiyan over the pass into Ghorband, at which time 650 tons of wheat from Ghazni would be sent to the southern Hazaras.

The WFP contingent, headed by a tall, acerbic, very funny Frenchman, hired the local Pushtun trucking mafia to haul the grain; the Pushtuns and their motley assortment of big trucks could deliver anything anywhere, across battlefields, national borders, and seemingly impassable mountains, for a price. They were the reason that Iranian Diet Cokes and fruit juice continued to show up in the Ghorband Bazaar, despite the fact that the valley was being blockaded by Taleban. After several hours of good-humored bargaining,

a price was agreed on, the trucks were loaded, and the next morning
we set out for Ghorband, the Frenchman and I following the caravan
in a WFP car with an Afghan driver. Within ten miles there were
three flat tires; then Doab, "Two Waters," where the road literally
ran through the stream bottom and the trucks lurched and groaned
through gravel banks and glacier melt; then the steep switchbacks
of Shebar, meadows and tundra grass and the hot blue sky, radiators
boiling over, and more flat tires; and finally, in the late afternoon,
through villages ravaged by fighting, a trashed tank, abandoned
trench lines, and the road junction where a right turn took you up
and over into the fairy-tale kingdom of Fendeckistan.

We spent the night with pro-Hazara *mujahedin*, and the next
morning we were promptly hijacked by a local bandit chief, a feck-
less little man who demanded all of the wheat, one truckload, a
few sacks, and finally nothing, when he discovered that the *muj*
up the road had captured two carloads of his men, beat them with
tree-limbs, and locked them in an underground dungeon.

A trade was agreed upon, safe passage for the wheat in return
for the release of the bandits and a promise from the *muj* not to
burn the chief's house down and shoot the occupants when they ran
out the door (their original plan for dealing with Mr. Bandit and
company).

The next day we drove out to the edge of No Man's Land. There
was a back-and-forth on the radio between the local pro-Hazara
commander and his counterpart on the Taleban side, and a few

minutes later a delegation of dark-clothed mullahs, thin as specters, appeared, and after brief negotiations the Frenchman, the driver, and I reboarded the WFP vehicle, and we led the column of trucks across the front lines into Talebanland.

Those first mullahs we met were quite friendly, but their boss, a tall, disdainful man, refused to shake hands with us, and didn't offer us tea, both terrible insults. He then ordered his men not to help unload the trucks—"to let the *kfirs* do it"; fortunately the truck drivers and locals pitched in to help. All well and good, except for the behavior of the Taleban toward the inhabitants of Ghorband. The wheat was supposed to be passed out among the locals regardless of ethnicity, but we immediately noticed that non-Pushtuns were being X-ed off the list of recipients: Taleban's members were 95 percent Pushtuns, but as the supposed legitimate government of the country the Talebs might have made at least a pretense of representing all Afghans—but no. And it became a moot point as we prepared to leave the next day: the Taleban had evidently decided that charity begins at home, and were confiscating the wheat from the townspeople and locking it up in a storehouse. We later heard that they put it up for sale on the open market.

But we had the last laugh after all. The Taleban chief, who had been so rude to us when we arrived and continued in the same vein the whole time we were there, must have gotten word from Kandahar to Kabul to be nice to us; when we stopped by his headquarters to say good-bye, he invited us in, and, *voilà*, there was a feast laid out:

pilaus, whole chickens, platefuls of grapes, piles of bread, lamb stew, potatoes, ravioli-like *mantou*.

I looked over at the Frenchman, and he looked at me; then he turned to the boss mullah: "I am so sorry, but you have been so hospitable to us since we arrived, we really cannot impose on you any further. Good day!"

We left him standing there, alone, with his unwanted feast.

A few days later, I got a ride in a UN jeep to Yawkalang, where a flight was leaving for Pakistan. As we pulled out of Bamiyan, I took a last look at the two Buddhas; I was planning on coming back in a month or two, to try and start some kind of low-profile aid project there, with Bamiyan University and some of the schools in the valley. I didn't know at the time that I was seeing the Buddhas for the last time; in fact, that I was the last American, and one of the last dozen or so Westerners, to see them standing.

A few weeks after I returned to the States, the Taleban and their al-Qaeda and Pakistani allies broke through the Hazaras' defenses to the south. Before they were through, every single building in Bamiyan was smashed or burned. The two great Buddhas were dynamited; Salafis in Pakistan published a bright color calendar of the final explosion, to celebrate the event. The students at Bamiyan University were massacred and their bodies stuffed down a well . . .

All without a real word of protest from the United States. Oh, there was the empty rhetoric of "we are concerned," "we view gravely," "that both sides refrain from . . ."—diplomatic code for "Let the slaughter go on . . ."

. . .

Meanwhile, of course, the preparations for the 9/11 attacks were going on; and it is clear to anyone who was in Afghanistan during the jihad against the Soviets and the Taleban era that there is no way they could have taken place without the knowledge, and perhaps the help, of high-level Saudi Arabians and ISI.

First of all, the money trail; it has been well-documented that Saudi money flowed to al-Qaeda and the hijackers themselves. But it led not only to Saudi Arabia, but Pakistan as well. One hundred thousand of the estimated half million dollars that paid for the operation was sent to Mohammed Atta, the leader of the hijacking teams, from a known Pakistani intelligence agent named Omar Syed Sheikh; the payment, via wire transfers from the United Arab Emirates, was personally authorized by General Mahmud Ahmed, then head of ISI. Mahmud was removed from his post the day after newspapers in India revealed his role in the 9/11 funding.

But the most compelling evidence is the relationship between ISI, al-Qaeda, and Taleban during the war with the Northern Alliance. *The three entities had no firewalls between them, no secrets; on the battlefield they operated as one*, ISI supplying fuel, transport, arms, ammunition, "volunteers," advisors, and air support when needed. When the Taleban had a particularly hard nut to crack militarily they called on al-Qaeda's elite Brigade O55, composed largely of Chechens, Algerians, Egyptians, and Saudis. When the U.S. fired sixty-six Tomahawk Cruise missiles at bin Laden's training camps outside Khost after the 1998 bombings of two U.S. embassies in Africa, we informed the Pakistani military in advance, as at least some of the missiles were going to pass through Pakistan's airspace. ISI promptly passed word to bin Laden—note that they had no problem contacting him on extremely short notice—and he was nowhere near the targeted sites when the missiles hit.

Obviously there were people in ISI and the Saudi money machine who knew what was going to come down on 9/11. Commander Ahmad Shah Massoud, Taleban and al-Qaeda's bitterest enemy, knew, through his own intelligence network in Afghanistan.

In fact, he made a special trip all the way to France, the only time he left Afghanistan in the twenty-three years since the Soviet invasion in 1979, solely to alert the West of the threat percolating in Afghanistan.

In a speech in Paris on April 6, 2001, he issued this blunt warning: "If President Bush doesn't help us, the terrorists [being trained in al-Qaeda camps in Taleban territory] will attack the U.S. and Europe very soon." In private, he was much more explicit. But Massoud had few friends in the CIA, which like most of official Washington cared little for Afghanistan other than as a convenient killing field for Russian troops. The hacks in Langley dismissed Massoud as a nuisance out of the past, and his warnings went into the "Outdated Intel/Doubtful Informant" file. After all, hadn't our good friends in Riyadh and Islamabad/Rawalpindi reassured us time and time again that they were in charge in Afghanistan, that the Taleban were no threat to anyone but themselves (and Massoud, along with a few soon-to-be extinct Hazaras), and to let well enough alone?

After all, bin Laden was eight thousand miles away in the mountains of Afghanistan, and the last time anyone checked al-Qaeda didn't have an air force. How were they going to attack America, with a fleet of magic carpets?

All along ISI has been extremely clever in persuading the media in the U.S. that Taleban was an entity independent of Pakistan, and that al-Qaeda somehow moved thousands of foreign fighters through Pakistan into Afghanistan without the permission or assistance of the Pakistani government; they had been clever, or perhaps it was that the American media was incredibly misinformed, lazy, and inept. It may be unfair to pick one example from so many, but one well-known journalist wrote about how he lobbied a magazine for month after month to send him to Afghanistan to report on the *mujahedin* and their war against the Soviets. When he finally went, he actually did a fine job, on a superficial level; but it was clear from his article that he had done *no* research, zero, on Afghanistan before he left: not a single book. His "background information" before he went in from Pakistan came from a drunken Britisher at the bar in the Intercon Hotel in Peshawar, who blathered about "proud Pathans" and such.

The most dramatic piece of proof about Pakistani and Taleban connivance in the 9/11 plot came with al-Qaeda's release of a video-tape in 2006 on the anniversary of the 9/11 attacks. In the tape, Osama bin Laden is shown discussing the plans for the attacks with Mohammed Atta, outdoors, in a crowded training camp in January 2000 with countless people within earshot. The idea that ISI was ignorant of such an important operation, one discussed so openly, is just plain nonsense.

Ahmad Shah Massoud was assassinated by a bomb concealed in a video camera in the northern Afghan town of Khvajeh Baha od Din two days before the 9/11 attacks, by two North African al-Qaeda members posing as journalists. My close friend Massoud Khalili, longtime aide to Massoud, was standing next to him, and he mirac-ulously survived, though he was in a coma for two weeks and suf-fered a shattered leg and a permanently injured eye. Massoud was killed in an attempt to sabotage any possible American retaliation for 9/11; without friendly Afghan fighters to work with and a liber-ated territory to base out of, we would have had an extremely dif-ficult task taking on Taleban and al-Qaeda. But for once luck was with us. The assassins were supposed to strike two weeks earlier, but they were stuck in a hotel in Tajikistan due to bad weather that had grounded Northern Alliance helicopters. In two weeks, the Taleban and their allies would have had time to bribe disillusioned, discouraged Northern Alliance commanders to their side and wrap up the last Alliance enclaves in the Panjshir Valley, the northern part of Hazaristan, Badakshan, and tiny pockets of Uzbeks loyal to Dostam in the Mazar-i-Sharif area.

Those two weeks made all the difference in the world. When the 9/11 attacks happened, it was instantly clear to the Northern Alliance forces that the U.S. would intervene in Afghanistan, and that their enemies' days were numbered: a 180-degree change in morale—and as Napoleon once said, morale is four times as important as all other factors combined in winning a battle or a war. Thus, the United States had a growing body of local anti-Taleban fighters and areas of liberated territory inside Afghanistan to work from when it went in to try and track down the authors of 9/11 and overthrow the regime that sheltered them. The fact that U.S. ground troops did not have to do 99 percent of the fighting was probably the major reason the war against Taleban/al-Qaeda went so smoothly.

When the U.S. finally intervened in Afghanistan in the wake of 9/11, both Saudi Arabia and Pakistan scurried to publicly distance themselves from both Taleban and al-Qaeda. The Pakistani government adopted a guise of "sympathetic interlocutor," urging the American government to hold off on a military response while the ISI rid Afghanistan of the "bad Taleban" with the aid of the "good Taleban," leaving the latter still in charge of the country. Assisted by the vociferous (and well-paid) Pakistan Lobby in Washington, composed mostly of retired U.S. diplomats formerly stationed in Islamabad, they came very close to succeeding. Only the courage of the few CIA agents already in Afghanistan—they had been helicoptered in soon after 9/11 to rally the anti-Taliban Northern Alliance to our side—forestalled the debacle. Led by two veteran operatives with extensive experience in Afghanistan, who knew just how devious Pakistan was and how determined they were to keep Afghanistan a puppet state, the CIA agents managed to convince the policy-makers in Washington that completely destroying the Taliban was the only way to root out al-Qaeda's presence on Afghan soil.

But in the end, ISI and al-Qaeda had the last laugh. As the Northern Alliance and its U.S. advisors, backed by American air power, swept across Afghanistan, the al-Qaeda retreated to two last redoubts: Osama bin Laden and several thousand hard-core foreign fighters holed up in the rock fortress of Tora Bora, west of the Khyber Pass, while in the north thousands of al-Qaeda and Taliban personnel and ISI officers found themselves surrounded in the town of Kunduz.

By now, most people are familiar with how bin Laden and his inner circle managed to escape from Tora Bora; the U.S. military foolishly entrusted local Afghan mercenaries and Pakistani Army troops with sealing off the escape routes into Pakistan, and they proceeded to do the exact opposite. The local Afghans charged a flat fee, payable in weapons or money, for each al-Qaeda member they escorted over the mountains to Pakistan, and once there the ISI helped them melt away into the tribal area of the North West Frontier Province, beyond the reach of U.S. intelligence. The full story is told later in this book.

The story of what happened at Kunduz is much less well known. According to U.S. Special Forces troops on the scene at the time, who were accompanying Northern Alliance forces as combat advisors, they were ready to move in on the encircled forces and kill or capture them. The parties trapped at Kunduz included some of the worst of the worst of America's enemies: al-Qaeda commanders and terrorist planners, Taliban commanders guilty of ethnically cleansing tens of thousands of Afghan civilians, and ISI officers who helped al-Qaeda function in Afghanistan and exfiltrate terrorists through Pakistan into the rest of the world.

But at the last minute, the SOF teams received new orders: the Pakistani government had asked the United States to allow I.S.I. personnel safe passage out of Kunduz, and someone back in Washington had agreed. The Americans and their Northern Alliance allies were ordered to pull back and let the enemy escape.

For the next three days, the Special Forces reined in their Afghan partners and ground their teeth in rage and frustration as Pakistani military transport planes shuttled people out of Kunduz: not the planeload or two of high-ranking ISI officers the Pakistanis had asked to be spared, but thousands of ISI troops, Arabs, Chechens, Algerians, a who's who of global terror, along with the Taleban leaders who would be sending suicide bombers back into Afghanistan three or four years later to kill American soldiers, leaders of the new Afghan government, civilian aid workers, and the like.

"Osama himself could have been on one of those planes," a Special Forces soldier said later, "and we never would have known. We had no control over who the goddamn Pakistanis flew out . . . people who knew who was really behind 9/11, people in charge of planning the next 9/11 . . . We had to just sit there and watch the planes fly out, day after day. Whoever okayed it in Washington was a stone traitor, as far as I'm concerned."

Which begs a last question: if ISI wasn't allied with al-Qaeda, why did Pakistan fly al-Qaeda personnel as well as ISI officers and Taleban commanders out of Kunduz in November 2001?

• • •

I was back in the United States, at my house in the Colorado Rockies, on September 11, 2001. I had gotten up early to watch CNN—this was back when CNN still covered significant world news stories, instead of happy talk, opinion, bloviating, and anything that can be filmed from a helicopter, no matter how trivial—a burning abandoned warehouse, a freeway chase in Dallas, or a hound dog being rescued from the ice of a frozen pond.

The first image I saw was one of the Twin Towers with a great smoking wound in its side; and a few moments later the second plane appeared—for some reason it looked black, funereal, a flying sarcophagus—seemed to pass behind the towers, do a sudden U-turn, and pierce the second tower like a spear, all the way through it, flames and debris exploding out the other side of the building. "Al-Qaeda," I thought instantly.

I returned to Afghanistan in time for the beginning of the end of Taleban rule, flying to Dushanbe, capital of Tajikistan, and traveling overland from there. The last time I had been in Afghanistan, there were three or four Western journalists based in-country, and maybe another half dozen, max, wandering the country on temporary assignment. Now there were close to a thousand either in Afghanistan or stuck in Pakistan or Tajikistan, trying to get in: sheer lunacy.

One group of hip young Turkish TV reporters had hauled their own satellite dish on a decrepit trailer towed behind a sedan all the way from Ankara. One large group had made it south to the Panjshiri Valley, where they were going stir-crazy waiting for the Northern Alliance to march on Kabul; their equipment was seizing up with the omnipresent dust, eggs were going for a buck each, seats on helicopters leaving the valley were selling for thousands, and desperate scriveners were actually slugging it out on the LZ, much to the amusement of the Panjshiri. I couldn't say I blamed the Afghans: everyone in the world had screwed them, they had suffered through two decades of war and the worst drought in the recorded history of Central Asia, and 99.9 percent of the global press was conspicuous by its absence through the whole hellish era.

Most of the rest were around Khvajeh Baha od Din, the Northern Alliance stronghold where Massood was assassinated two days before 9/11. That was where I ended up; my old friend Don North (he had been Morley Safer's cameraman in Vietnam!) rented a car and driver south to the Amu Darya, crossed the river by night on a primitive ferry, and then hired a Jeep for an exorbitant fee for the twenty minute drive to town.

Khvajeh Baha od Din presented a strange, strange scene. Taleban and al-Qaeda forces were entrenched on the ridgeline to the south-west, while the town was booming thanks to the horde of cash-heavy journalists stranded there. Each of the various American television networks had leased the largest house and compound they could find, except for one that was actually having a gigantic house *built* for them. There were special truck convoys every week from Dushanbe, carrying steaks, ice cream, Evian, imported premium beer, whiskey, CDs, and DVDs.

What was really remarkable was how ignorant most of the press was. Almost all of them had somehow gotten the idea that the Northern Alliance was headed by drug smugglers and "warlords," and that their soldiers were reluctant to fight. To take the first point: when a people are facing genocide and no one is helping them—in fact, when countries like the United States are in effect aiding and abeting the genocide—taxing drug exports to buy the means of survival is hardly the most heinous crime imaginable. And whatever "warlords" there were in Afghanistan were created by the way ISI and other groups supplied weapons to their favorite commanders; warlords are not an intrinsically Afghan phenomenon. And if the Northern Alliance commanders and their men wanted to wait for American air power to soften up the enemy before attacking, consider this: most of the older *mujahedin* by now had been fighting nonstop for twenty years, first against the Soviets, then against other *mujahedin*, then against Pakistan, foreign Moslems, and Taleban, while the younger ones had never known anything but war, and had been fighting since they were eleven or twelve. One young Hazara commander described his heartbreaking life to two British cameramen: "I joined up to kill. Once my parents killed, I killed often. Afghans fight. I fight." Why would anyone weary and sick of an endless war want to die unnecessarily at the very end of the conflict?

The problem was, 95 percent of the American journalists covering the final act of the war between the Northern Alliance and Taleban had never been in Afghanistan before, knew next to nothing about the country, and really didn't seem to want to know. Most weren't sure what a Hazara was, or a Shi'a, or what a map of Afghanistan looked like: I heard one network talking head refer to "the city of Jalalabad, midway between Kabul and Kandahar," akin to talking about "Nashville, on the road from New York to Washington, D.C." Afghans are the best interview subjects in the world, voluble, eloquent, eager to talk, but one almost never heard the voices of Afghan people during the war against Taleban, or even got to see them: the classic American TV report was a screen filled by a reporter in body armor, talking about his idea of what was going on on the battlefield (with an emphasis on his own courage), with sounds of war someplace far, far in the distance. Often the armored talking head whispered dramatically, as if Osama bin Laden and Ramzi Youssef were ten feet away in an adjoining foxhole. Most of it was useless, and much of the rest downright pernicious. In the end, the general picture you got was of the American military avenging 9/11, accompanied by a corps of heroic correspondents, while the faceless, voiceless, dilatory and halfhearted soldiers of the corrupt Northern Alliance tried to avoid battle with the faceless, nameless, wrongheaded but courageous fighters of Taleban. If the latter had a major flaw, according to the media, it was that they were misogynists, like Republican evangelicals only worse; no mention of ethnic cleansing, like the depopulation of the Shomali Plain north of Kabul, 90,000 Tajik civilians driven out or killed, or the mass slaughter of Hazara men and boys in the streets of Mazar-i-Sharif, or the total depopulation and destruction of the ancient town of Bamiyan. And no mention of the fact that by the time of 9/11 close to half of Taleban's front-line fighters were non-Afghans, Pakistanis and al-Qaeda types, and young Pushtuns, the tribal group that founded Taleban, had to be recruited by force or paid to fight.

The ignorance of the American media played a major role in turning what should have been a war of moderate Moslems, aided by the U.S., against the violent, atavistic minority attempting to hijack the faith, into the so-called "War on Terror," in which *we* were going to "clean up" Islam, deciding who the good and bad Moslems were along the way: the old, old story of ignorance begetting disaster.

My friend Don North and I never made it down south to see the liberation of Kabul, but we did get to witness the end of Taleban rule in the northwest. The second morning we were in Khvajeh Baha od Din I was walking through the center of town when I noticed that everyone was looking up at the sky; I followed their gaze and saw the unmistakeable contrails of three B-52s, looping back toward the south. Because of their extreme altitude and speed, and their distance from the target, they seemed to have nothing at all to do with the Taleban/al-Qaeda positions nearby; but the bombs were already falling, angling, on their computer-preordained path, and a few seconds later the enemy ridgeline began to explode, without a sound: one towering mushroom after another, of earth, smoke, powdered stone, vaporized flesh, weaponry, in a perfect line, until the entire top of the ridge was obliterated.

The whole time, schoolkids were dancing around me, cheering, laughing, hugging my knees. Khvajeh Baha od Din was mostly a Tajik, Uzbek, and Turkoman town, like most of northern Afghanistan, and the people there knew well what they could expect if the enemy captured it, particularly from the Arabs and the other foreign Moslems. Everywhere they had gone they had commited unspeakable atrocities, torching mosques and Korans, raping children, staging mass throat-cuttings of prisoners; their cruelty after capturing Yawkalang, north of Bamiyan, was so extreme that the Taleban began fighting against their foreign Moslem allies to get them to stop (the Arabs were hanging civilians from power lines, carving away prisoners' faces till they slowly died, burning people alive, etc.).

A couple of days later, Don and I decided to risk traveling to Faizabad, in the foothills of Badakshan province, in the far north-western corner of Afghanistan. I had visited there a couple of years ago, flying in on a UN flight. Then it had been a rear area of the war: the front lines were west of Taloqan, the de facto capital of the Northern Alliance, which in turn was west of Faizabad; since then Taloqan had been captured by Taleban, aided by Pakistani air strikes, leaving only Khvajeh Baha od Din, Faizabad, and the Panjshir Valley, each in its own isolated pocket, free of Taleban domination.[4] People in Khvajeh Baha od Din were saying that Taloqan was on the verge of being liberated by the Northern Alliance, so it seemed like a good place to go.

We hired a classic mashed Soviet Army jeep with a high-spirited young Tajik driver, a hundred dollers including gas for the whole trip (one way), and headed southeast out of Khvajeh Baha od Din. There was a certain amount of peril to the journey: the Taleban/al-Qaeda forces in northwest Afghanistan were holing up in Kunduz to make a

---

[4] There was actually a rough dirt track over the high mountains from Faizabad to the Upper Panjshir Valley, open only for a few weeks each summer. Aside from helicopter flights from Dushanbe, that was the Panjshir's only link with the out-side world at the time Massood was assassinated; from Faizabad, there was an extremely rough overland route into the mountains of eastern Tajikistan, used mostly by drug smugglers.

last stand, but some were fleeing to the south, trying to make it back over the Salang to Kabul and on to Kandahar; the foreign Moslems especially had no illusions about their fate if they were captured, considering the war crimes they had committed (I ran into some Panjshiri friends in Kabul a few months later, and some had pocketfuls of Saudi Arabian passports, credit cards, and the like. When I asked where they got them, they told me that they had trapped two thousand hard-core enemy fighters, many of them foreigners, just south of the Salang. Some they saved to sell to the Americans—the asking price was two or three thousand U.S. dollars—but many they didn't want to trouble themselves with, and so—they flashed a grin, drew a finger across their throat, and made that sound effect, something like a zipper being pulled. Most of the passports were Saudi Arabian, and the faces inside were those of young men, well-to-do looking, with neatly combed beards and deadpan expressions; you could imagine them skiing at Aspen, playing roulette in Malaysia, or going 140 on the autobahn in a Mercedes.

At any rate, if we ran into any fleeing Talebs or foreign fighters, we would be dead meat. There was also an unbelievable yet somehow disturbing story going around that bin Laden had built a sprawling underground fortress by the Amu Darya—tens of thousands of trucks worth of concrete and rebar, complete with lights, computer banks, ventilation—and I kept having his terrible vision, of bin Laden and Zawahiri like two trap-door spiders who would suddenly pop out, snare us, and pull us back underground with them, where we would never see the light of day again. The story was ridiculous, of course, a bad James Bond riff, but so was the reality of that world: a six-foot-five, murderous Arab millionaire, second cousin of Fu Manchu, obsessed with poisons and deadly viruses, able to appear and disappear like a djinn. I had been dodging and jousting out here for way too long, at the edge of that weird, dark world; after a while you became as paranoid and obsessive as the enemy. Just two nights before I had dreamed I was guiding an Army SOF team on bin Laden's trail; we raced down a slot canyon maybe two feet wide and a thousand feet deep in near-darkness, and every hundred feet or so we found another lump of green, glowing enriched uranium, dropped by bin Laden; he was leading us on, deeper and deeper into the Underworld, Jehannum, the Land of the Dead . . .

> Imagine a person tall, lean and feline, high-shouldered, with a brow like Shakespeare and a face like Satan, a close-shaven skull, and long, magnetic eyes of true cat-green. Invest him with all the cruel cunning of an entire Eastern race, accumulated in one giant intellect, with all the resources of science, past and present, with all the resources, if you will, of a wealthy government—which, however, already has denied all knowledge of his existence. . . . This man, whether a fanatic or a duly appointed agent is, unquestionably, the most malign and formidable personality existing in the world today. . . . He has the brains of any three men of genius. . . . Imagine that awful being, and you have a mental picture of Dr. Fu-Manchu, the yellow peril incarnate in one man.
>
> —Sax Rohmer, *The Mystery of Dr. Fu-Manchu*, 1936

The drive to Faizabad was epic. Part of the way we followed what had been the main road connecting Badakshan with the rest of Afghanistan: over muddy hills, crumbling switchbacks down rocky slopes; at one point the roadway was actually a whitewater stream you could have run a kayak slalom through, with wrecked trucks on their sides or upside down everywhere. We had no idea where we were on the map 'til suddenly we were driving through the town of Rostaq, on a green mesa top; there had been a major earthquake there in 1998 that killed as many as six thousand people and had made the news worldwide. Poor Afghanistan, you navigated across it from one disaster or atrocity site to another: here a thousand Taleban prisoners were killed by Uzbeks, here a valley with ten or twenty thousand inhabitants was totally depopulated by Taleban/al-Qaeda, here a plague killed half the children, here an avalanche or mudslide wiped out two entire villages . . . the country was a map of miseries, most of them visited upon the innocent . . . a geography of endless suffering and sorrow.

We reached Faizabad in the early evening, and rented a room in one of the guest houses overhanging the river. The town had prospered off the opium and heroin trade, and the bazaar was full of cheap TVs, cassette players, boomboxes, and cheap synthetic double-breasted suits from some warehouse in Eastern Europe; men and boys roared around in 4WD Toyota pickups and on motorbikes, and several strains of Indian film music and Afghan traditional pop blasted from music stores.

Everyone was talking happily about Taleban's downfall, and there was a rowdy festival feeling in the air. The town was full of refugees from Taloqan, anxiously awaiting word that the Bad Guys had been killed or had fled from their town; they were already packed for the journey home over the mountains.

The next night the news came, like an explosion: the Taleban and their foreign allies were gone from Taloqan, fleeing south, desperately trying to escape the vengeance of the local people, or retreating toward Kunduz to make a last stand. Faizabad erupted in what Afghans call "happy firing": a tank's main gun opened up over the rooftops of town, one, two thunderous shots; countless heavy machine guns sprayed the sky with tracers from hilltop outposts; Kalashnikovs on full auto ripped everywhere; across the river someone was lobbing rockets from an RPG out across the dark landscape. Less than five minutes after the news arrived the main street of town was full of big trucks, overloaded with families from Taloqan and their belongings; they couldn't wait till the next morning to go home. One by one they lurched off into the dark, for the hazardous passage over the mountains.

Early the next morning I was walking down by the river when I ran into three teenaged schoolgirls. All of them were wearing the all-encompassing shrouds called burkahs. Contrary to the ideas of Western feminists, burkahs had not always been a symbol of gender oppression in Afghanistan; when I visited the country in the early 70s, they were very much the vogue among middle- and upper-class urban women, to indicate how genteel and ultrafeminine they were;

village women usually wore a simple shawl covering their hair. Of course, when it became mandatory under the Taleban, what had been fashion became tyranny. It's like the old hotel/jail equation: lock someone up in a luxury hotel for five years, never let them leave, and it becomes an unbearable prison.

As I said my "asalaam aleikums" and began to pass the three girls, the tallest and boldest stepped forward, lifted her burkah exposing her face, and looked at me straight in the eyes before lowering the cloth and leading her two friends past me. That wordless gesture said everything there was to say about Taleban.

CHAPTER 7

ICEBERGS IN THE FOG

In November 2001, as anti-Taleban Afghans and their American advisors and allies captured more and more territory, Osama bin Laden and his inner circle of advisors, along with their elite foreign Moslem bodyguards, gathered in the city of Jalalabad, near the western end of the Khyber Pass. The surrounding area had been a longtime al-Qaeda stronghold, with terrorist training camps and bases at Hadda Farm, Tora Bora, and on the shores of the reservoir west of town.

In his book *Al-Qaeda's Great Escape*, correspondent Philip Smucker does a brilliant job of reconstructing the bin Laden's last days before disappearing; Smucker traveled to Jalalabad less than two weeks after Osama vanished, and interviewed eyewitnesses while their memories were still fresh.

On November 9, Taleban leaders in Jalalabad called for a mass meeting of tribal chiefs from Afghanistan's eastern border mountains, and mobilized a corps of minivans to bring them to the big building housing al-Qaeda's Islamic Studies Institute, in the center of the city. A thousand or more chiefs showed up, and the afternoon of the ninth found them crowded into the institute's basement, sitting Afghan-style on the floor, enjoying a feast of lamb and rice with all the trimmings. In the midst of the meal one of the al-Qaeda Arabs among the diners announced the arrival of a "special guest," and a few moments later bin Laden appeared, surrounded by more than a dozen armed bodyguards.

According to Smucker's informant, one of the Afghan tribal leaders in attendance that night, the crowd pelted bin Laden with flowers as the Arabs among them led the Afghans in cheers and anti-American chants. Bin Laden spoke briefly, asking the chiefs for their help in fighting the Americans and their Afghan allies, and then sat down to dine. Less than forty-five minutes later he rose suddenly and exited with his guards and a group of senior Taleban leaders, but not before his Arab underlings went through the crowd handing out envelopes full of Pakistani rupees. If Smucker's informant is to be believed, the payments were hardly lavish: big tribal bosses get ten thousand dollars or more, while minor village clan leaders like the informant received something like three hundred: not much for being bombed with daisycutters, fuel-air, and cluster bombs dropped by B-52s.

For the next three days, bin Laden and his al-Qaeda inner circle remained in Jalalabad, most likely as guests of Mohammed Yunis Khalis, the aged Afghan mullah and onetime *mujahedin* chief who was one of his most fervent local supporters and an enthusiastic supporter of Taleban. Bin Laden himself stayed discretely out of sight, no doubt worried about being spotted by an American spy satellite or reconnaissance drone and finding himself on the receiving end of a Hellfire air-to-surface missile. Meanwhile hundreds more foreign al-Qaeda fighters gathered in the city, virtually taking it over, as bombs fell on known al-Qaeda/Taleban installations and even hardcore local Taleban supporters grew increasingly uneasy about the fate of their city.

At some point during this time bin Laden must have begun to realize that his dinner guests on the ninth were not rallying their tribesmen to battle the approaching infidels. The late Professor Louis Dupree, who knew Afghanistan and its people intimately, used to say, "You can rent an Afghan, but you can't buy him." Unless they are fighting for their own honor, land, and faith, the Afghans tend to be instinctual pragmatists. No matter how loudly they had cheered him at the banquet on the ninth, through mouths stuffed with his pilau and kebabs, they were now talking amongst themselves, with considerably less interest in fighting to the death for a young Arab's visions.

On the night of the thirteenth, a local guest house owner named Babrak watched as a convoy of vehicles, as many as two hundred of them, formed up outside his gate. There were scores of new white Pajeros, jammed with armed Chechens, Arabs, and other foreign fighters, more four-wheel drive pickups full of al-Qaeda fighters, as well as five armored vehicles. Barbrak and his neighbor watched as Osama got out of his customized Corolla hatchback and joined a group of the top Taleban leaders from Jalalabad. They conferred for a few minutes, evidently debating whether the Taleban and al-Qaeda forces should stay in the city and attempt to defend it against the American-led forces when they arrived. Finally discretion outweighed valor, and the convoy mounted up and headed out, departing Jalalabad on the network of rough dirt roads that lead west northwest, toward Tora Bora, a heavily fortified cave complex in the foothills of the Safed Koh, the White Mountains.

The intrepid Smucker found another informant, the headman of a village along the route to Tora Bora, who provided the last solid account of bin Laden's movements. According to him, bin Laden and his inner circle arrived in the village late at night on the thirteenth, and stopped to confer with the headman and the village elders. It seems clear from the headman's account, confirmed by others who were there, that by this time the tribesmen around Jalalabad were weighing their choices and deciding that the ancient Pushtun tradition of self-interest prevailed. Bin Laden and company "donated" four hundred brand-new AK-47s to the villagers, in return for which they agreed to help spirit al-Qaeda leaders and their families across the mountains to Pakistan if and when the situation at Tora Bora became hopeless. The wily villagers would be charging a hefty fee for each fugitive, of course. Many of them had attended the feast on November 9, where they had greeted bin Laden with a rain of flowers and shouted "Death to America! Death to Israel!" alongside his al-Qaeda cheerleaders; but now the Sheikh (bin Laden's favorite title) and his followers were just another foreign army, down on its luck in the mountains of Afghanistan, *their* mountains, and to the headman and the villagers they must have looked like so many gunny-sacks full of ten-rupee notes, just waiting to be grabbed.

The conference over, bin Laden and his companions left the village, joining the horde of warriors, supporters, and their families, spreading out through the tunnels and caves honeycombing the black cliffs of Tora Bora.

In the days that followed, U.S. Army Special Forces "A" Teams showed up in Jalalabad and recruited a small mercenary army of local tribesmen to besiege Tora Bora. B-52s deluged the cave fortifications with bombs, including ground-penetrating "bunker-busters," fuel-air explosives that sucked the oxygen out of the deepest hidden redoubts, and huge daisy cutters, whose blast eradicated everything across an area the size of twenty football fields. In a few cases the hired tribesmen got close enough to the al-Qaeda forces to kill or be killed, but for the most part the battle was fought with total impunity from high in the air.

Meanwhile, as the inexorable destruction went on, a steady stream of refugees, wounded fighters, camp followers, women, and children trickled through the encircling tribesmen and paid their way to safety in Pakistan over the remote back trails known only to smugglers, nomads, and local herdsmen. The same local villagers who had sworn to fight alongside al-Qaeda now profited from their erstwhile allies' defeat, charging al-Qaeda members as much as fifty thousand Pakistani rupees apiece to guide them through the frontlines to safety.

The fugitives moved along two main routes, called "ratlines" by the U.S. military and CIA. One led east of Jalalabad, then north across the main highway to the Khyber Pass, crossing the Kabul River by ferry at the bombed-out village of Lalitpur; from there it was an easy journey up the Kunar River valley and across the mountains into Pakistan via Nawa Pass, the same route Alexander the Great's armies had taken in 327 BC on their way to India. The second followed the old *mujahedin* supply lines east by southeast, through the heart of the Safed Koh: it entered Pakistan either at the smugglers' haunt of Terri Mangal, or further south, crossing the hills east of Khost to the Pakistani town of Miram Shah.

It was almost a miracle that anyone survived at Tora Bora, where the bombing was a hundred times more intense than what I saw at Khvajeh Baha od Din, and went on day after day for weeks. When the US-backed tribal mercenaries finally entered Tora Bora in mid-December, they found only two dozen or so shell-shocked, half-dead al-Qaeda fighters huddled here and there in the shattered tunnels and caves. But of bin Laden and the other al-Qaeda leaders, there was no sign.

Up through the time Tora Bora was finally occupied, the CIA, the U.S. military, and the Bush administration in Washington, D.C., had continued to boast that bin Laden was trapped in his doomed stronghold, with no place to go; either that, or he was already dead, blown to bits, or entombed deep in some subterranean lair. But as the fog of war began to lift, a different scenario emerged.

Bin Laden's exact movements during the siege remain a mystery. All that is known is that on the evening of November 26, Osama and three companions showed up at a cave emplacement occupied by a group of hard-core Yemeni, al-Qaeda fighters. Osama was drinking a glass of green tea, and appeared calm, as if he felt perfectly safe and secure. He urged the Yemenis to keep fighting until they were martyred, and to kill as many of the infidels as they could before they died. And then he and his three comrades left, walking east into the gathering darkness, heading into the high jumbled peaks of the Safed Koh and the safety of Pakistan, two or three days away.

This was the last time anyone saw the head of al-Qaeda, the architect of 9/11 and the world's most wanted man. Four or five days later American Special Forces troops reportedly overheard Osama on a satellite phone giving instructions to his followers at Tora Bora, and it was taken as evidence that he was still on the scene, directing the fighting; but now it is believed that if it was really bin Laden's voice on the phone he was calling from the safety of Pakistan; or else that the voice on the phone was a recording, a clever piece of disinformation to throw bin Laden's pursuers off his trail.

When the siege of Tora Bora began, I was back in the States again; and as I followed the story, and it became clear that Osama had escaped, I began to get a funny feeling; and the longer bin Laden stayed invisible, totally and completely unaccounted for, the funnier

I felt. Something just didn't compute. It was that classic old story of
the Dog That Didn't Bark in the Night . . .

According to both the intelligence community and the media,
bin Laden ended up in the Tribal Area of Pakistan's North West
Frontier Province, where his tribal allies gave him shelter. And
there he remains to this day, either cowering in a cave or living as
a virtual prisoner within the high walls of one of the thousands of
fortified compounds that dot the area. Bin Laden had longstand-
ing ties with the Pushtun tribes in the NWFP, particularly those
living between Terri Mangal and Miram Shah. He had operated
a highly lucrative heroin smuggling business from Afghanistan
into Pakistan in partnership with them; and they were close kin to
the Pushtun tribes in southern and eastern Afghanistan, who had
made up almost all of the membership of the Taleban movement.
It would have made perfect sense for the Pushtuns of the NWFP
to protect bin Laden, even after the United States government
announced it was offering a $25 million reward for him, dead or
alive . . .

But something bothered me: the fact that more and more time
went by without a single sighting of the al-Qaeda leader, or even
the vaguest rumor of his whereabouts. To hear the "experts" talk, the
NWFP is as unknowable as the dark side of the moon, a time-warp
realm, "wilder than the wild, wild West," (if you believe President
Bush) in which secrets are kept forever and outsiders never find out
what is really going on. But unlike the "experts," I had spent a lot

of time in the NWFP; and to me, it didn't make sense, not at all. It seemed to me that one could start from there and make a pretty good deduction about just where bin Laden was, and who was doing such a perfect job of hiding him . . .

• • •

During the war against the Soviets, I had ended up spending a lot of time in the Federally Administered Tribal Area of the NWFP; almost all of the covert routes into eastern Afghanistan crossed the tribal area either north or south of the Khyber Pass. Inevitably, I had gotten to know many of the people and places along the Pakistan-Afghanistan border that now loom so large in news coverage of the War on Terror: the resurgent Afghan Taleban, the new Pakistani Taleban, and the search for bin Laden, Ayman ak-Zawahiri, and the rest of the illusive al-Qaeda leadership.

The FATA is a hard place for outsiders to operate in, but it is hardly the impenetrable, unknowable "Dark Side of the Moon" Djinistan that many in the media and in our government portray. The truth is, it is one of the most intensely researched regions in South Asia, thanks to the British; in their efforts to safeguard the western borders of their Indian empire and pacify the restive tribes there, they scrutinized every last little detail about it, from geography, hydrology, geology, botany, and climatology to ethnohistory, theology, mythology, linguistics, and agronomy. The Political Agents, the political/diplomatic arm of British governance (the other arm, of course, was military), knew the ways of the country and its people inside out; read the voluminous records they left, and you understand exactly how they kept the peace with a minimum of bloodshed. They could outride, outshoot, and outfight the toughest tribesmen on the frontier, crack jokes and make puns in colloquial Pushtu, and sniff out the sneakiest ambush in advance.

The point is this, the area where bin Laden is almost certainly living—"hiding" is a misleading term, when those looking for you haven't a clue about what they are doing—is not concealed in some impenetrable Cloud of Unknowing. When I wrote an article on the Khyber Pass for *Smithonian Magazine* in the 1980s, I had no problem visiting Nadir Khan Zakhakhel, the courtly tribal chief and co-czar of the billion-dollar smuggling business between Afghanistan and Pakistan; in fact, we became such good friends that he once rescued me from being hauled off to jail by the Khyber Rifles at Torkham Khyber, after I had been detained for illegally crossing the border. Western journalists were always welcome guests in Nadir Khan's mile-long high-walled compound, with its marble mosque, huge rose garden (tended by no fewer than fifty gardeners), remote-opened and -closed windows with twenty-four carat gold frames, and fleet of forty Mercedes limousines. Once I even crossed the supposedly forbidden Tirah Valley, of which it was said "No infidel shall sleep the night here and be alive in the morning." Other foreigners far more fluent in Pushtu who spent much longer periods in the FATA were allowed to visit sites as sacrosanct as a Pushtun clan's subterranean heroin factory, where Chinese-trained tribal chemists converted masses of raw opium paste into morphine base and then the much more lucrative tan heroin known as "Number Two" in the global narco-trade.

Much has been made of the case of the Fakir of Ipi, the anti-British Pushtun guerrilla leader who evaded capture or killing for decades up on the frontier and finally died peacefully of old age in 1960; the British lost hundreds if not thousands of men in their unsuccessful fight against him. But this doesn't explain the present case of bin Laden's success in evasion in the same region.

1. The Fakir of Ipi commanded an army of as many as three thousand fighters in an area he and they knew in detail, in an era before spy satellites, helicopters, and unmanned surveillance drones.
2. The British almost always knew approximately where he was, they just couldn't apprehend him.
3. The Fakir of Ipi was not a six-foot-five Arab traveling with a group of Chechen bodyguards, with a price of $50 million on his head.

The more time that went by without even the rumor of a sighting of bin Laden, the more uncomfortable I became with the facile explanation that he was "being protected by the Pushtun tribes in the area," for all the reasons above. There's probably never been a place with *fewer* secrets than the tribal area of the North West Frontier Province.

People love to talk in the NWFP, they talk about *everything*, and it all ends up in the bazaars and teahouses, as far away as Peshawar, Kabul, and the Pushtun colonies in Karachi and London.

Whenever I'm in Afghanistan I ask my friends there about the idea of bin Laden remaining invisible in the FATA for years and years and they laugh and laugh:

> If he was in some villager's compound, the women in the family would have been complaining at the village well after a few days: 'Those Chechens are eating everything in the house; those Arabs expect tea all night long, and then they complain it's not as good as in Riyadh.' And the men, they would all be bragging the day after he arrived, 'Guess who I have in my compound? The American infidels can't buy me, not for fifty, for a hundred million dollars!' Village kids would say, 'Let's walk past Habibullah's house and see if we see one of the Chechens, or the Tall Arab!' And then someone in the village would say to himself, 'I know Habibullah's getting paid to hide the Tall Arab—thousands of *lakhs* of rupees—and he's already so rich!' Why didn't the Arab stay in Saudi Arabia, where he belongs? He'll just bring trouble to everyone here, the longer he stays—

If he isn't living with the people in the NWFP, then where is he? Well, consider this thought: Only a state intelligence agency could provide the total invisibility that bin Laden has enjoyed for the last several years. Like ISI, for instance, or some major elements thereof, both active duty and "retired." Just a hunch, but if I were ISI, I wouldn't want my guest on Pakistan soil; if by some chance things unraveled and his whereabouts came out, I would want at least some plausible deniability as to my involvement. I would want to be "Extraordinary Rendition"—and Gitmo-proof, if at all possible.

The safest place to put him would be just across the border in Afghanistan. There are rumors that the Pakistani military has had highly secret installations there for some time; part of their obsession with "Strategic Depth," created by the fact that their country's vital center, site of Islamabad, Rawalpindi, and Lahore, is so narrow; an Indian armored thrust could cut the country in two, all the way west to the Khyber Pass, in less than a day. Some think the Pakistanis have even located a percentage of their last retaliatory resources, their nuclear-armed cruise missiles, there, beyond the gaze of Indian intelligence; if the enemy can't account for some of your deadliest weapons, they are a lot less likely to mount an attack. Why not hide your most precious secrets, including bin Laden, where no one would ever look?

Of course, it would have to be a part of Afghanistan accessible to Pakistan, but almost unreachable from anywhere else west of the border . . .

• • •

Bin Laden is just one piece of the menace we are confronted by. We had never faced an enemy like al-Qaeda before: it is something entirely new under the sun, a hybrid entity with the fanatical indestructibility and impenetrable opacity of a religious cult and the ability of a multinational corporation to innovate and expand, able to morph into a thousand forms that feed on local grievances.

If one wanted to find a historical example of a covert religious organization similar to al-Qaeda, the Assassins are a perfect fit. A subsect of Shi'ism, it was founded in the mid-eleventh century by Hassan-i-Sabbah, "the Old Man of the Mountain." Based in the remote mountains of northern Iran, the group quickly became notorious for its killings of Sunni Moslem leaders who opposed the sect. For more than two hundred years, no one who opposed Hassan-i-Sabbah and his successors was safe, from Iran to Egypt. The Assassins were highly skilled in "deep cover" tradecraft; trained to speak foreign languages fluently, they successfully impersonated merchants, peasants, and soldiers from all over the Middle East, and infiltrated the inner circles of the most closely guarded throne rooms of their foes. When they succeeded in getting close to their victims they struck quickly, with ritual daggers, and then made no effort to escape, choosing martyrdom for their faith. The Sunni leader Nizam al-Mulk was killed on his way to visit his harem by an Assassin disguised as a Sufi holy man; the former caliph (head of the Sunni faith) al-Rashid was killed by four Assassins who had succeeded in joining his corps of bodyguards. One anti-Assassin Sunni leader decided to make peace with them when he awoke in the middle of his armed camp to find a dagger driven into the ground next to him and a note from Hassan-i-Sabbah telling him the knife could have just as easily been planted in his heart. Another caliph discovered that his children's beloved longtime tutor was an Assassin agent. In a very real sense, the Assassins were the world's first terrorists: they believed that a few choice killings, carried out by agents who were impossible to identify and therefore thwart, were much more effective than mass slaughter in spreading fear.

Like al-Qaeda, the Assassins were completely immune to penetration from the outside: only the cult's leaders knew the group's secrets and plans. Like al-Qaeda, the group's operatives were totally prepared to die carrying out their leaders' orders. They also relied on terror itself as a weapon against its enemies: as one Assassin leader wrote, "[B]y one single warrior on foot a king may be stricken with terror, though he own more than a hundred thousand horsemen." After 9/11, Osama bin Laden used almost identical language when he boasted of how a few young Moslem men managed to shake the mightiest nation on earth and cost it tens of billions of dollars in economic damage.

In al-Qaeda's case, ancient ways like those of the Assassins are combined with twenty-first century technology and advertising techniques. Using both the Internet and media outlets like al-Jazeera's global television news network, al-Qaeda has found a way to endlessly replicate itself, forming what are in effect franchises without ever directly contacting the franchisees. They accomplish this with three kinds of communications. The first consists of a constant blizzard of news/propaganda chronicling the sufferings of Moslems at the hands of America, Israel, and their allies and cohorts in Russia, India, and other countries. Second, jihadis around the world put out hundreds of

Internet videos of attacks on anti-Moslem forces, bombings, snipings, and ambushes, with soundtracks of rousing Arabic resistance songs: these serve both as inspiration to potential terrorists and insurgents around the world, and as instructional material. They are notably effective on both levels. When I was in Baghdad with the 425th Civil Affairs Battalion in 2004, a video showed up on the Internet of a Chechen car bomb attack on a Russian convoy: a car parked along the road was loaded with explosives, and when a column of military vehicles passed by it was detonated. Within a week, VBIEDs, Vehicle Borne Improvised Explosives Devices, began showing up in Iraq.

Then there are the terrorist instruction manuals al-Qaeda has assembled and published online. They include material from such diverse sources as the 1960s countercultural icon *The Anarchist Cookbook,* U.S. Army Field Manuals, and chemistry textbooks; how-to sections on setting up terrorist cells, making explosives and poisons, carrying out hit and run assassinations, establishing false identities, acquiring and training with small arms; "and much, much more," as the ad writers say: a total of over 1,100 pages of deadly information.

Given what al-Qaeda has made available on the Internet and in the media, a Moslem youth anywhere on earth can be politically radicalized, informed of the existence of successful jihadi insurgent and terrorist groups around the world, and given the training to join the jihad himself, all without ever meeting a live al-Qaeda recruiter or propagandist.

In addition, al-Qaeda has shown a unique ability to bond symbiotically with other kinds of organizations, ranging from factions within state intelligence agencies to the huge international criminal enterprises that have sprung up in the brave new world of globalization. The latter are particularly useful in moving people, weapons, and other materiel from country to country. The same kinds of ratlines that smuggle stolen antiquities, sex slaves, Chinese acetyl anhydride into Tajikistan to manufacture heroin, the finished heroin into Iran or Albania, or tax-free cigarettes from North Carolina through the Mohawk Nation to Montreal,[5] can move the chief of Al-Qaeda in Uzbekistan and his carry-on nuke from a weapons

---

[5] Until recently, a Middle Eastern immigrant gang ran a highly lucrative business trucking semi-loads of tax-free cigarettes directly from the warehouses in North Carolina into Canada for the Montreal French-Canadian Mafia; the cigarettes were then marketed through small mom-and-pop convenience stores throughout Quebec. The smugglers got past the U.S.-Canadian border via the Mohawk Nation, the large Native American preservation reservation that straddles the border. The Mohawk Nation has its own justice system and police force, and the people tend to violently resist outside interference in their affairs by "white" law enforcement or anyone else. In addition, the local topography, with its maze of lakes and islands, makes surveillance and interdiction of contraband almost impossible. Members of the Pushtun tribe, these truckers have a history of allying themselves with the movement. In fact, the first time Taleban appeared on the battlefield was in early November 1994, when a band of Taleban fighters liberated a Central Asia–bound convoy of Pakistani trucks with Pushtun drivers that had been seized by renegade *mujahedin* while driving through the Kandahar area, in southern Afghanistan.

Today, if you paid a Pushtun truck driver enough money, he would run your cargo, licit or illicit, from Turkmenistan all the way across Afghanistan to the eastern borders of Pakistan. And some say their turf doesn't end there: greased with enough baksheesh for the authorities, they could keep going, across the border into India, or over the Khunjerab Pass into the far western reaches of China.

cache in the mountains of Paktika Province in Afghanistan to
Turkmenistan, on to Albania, then Mexico, and across the *frontera*
to Your Town, U.S.A.

And al-Qaeda can call on a host of allies and confederates around
the world:

1. The Pushtun trucking mafia in Afghanistan and Pakistan:
   Descendants of the nomad caravan masters of the past, the
   long-haul truckers from the Pushtun tribe have controlled
   commerce in Afghanistan for decades. During the Soviet-
   Afghan war, when millions of Afghans fled to Pakistan, the
   Pushtun truckers came with them, and by the end of the war
   they virtually ran Pakistan's road transport system all the way
   from the Khunjerab Pass in the far north to Karachi in the
   south. In addition to legitimate cargo-hauling, they have been
   notorious for their role in smuggling drugs, weapons, and
   anything else profitable. Because the Taleban are dominated
   by Pushtuns, they have an inside track with the mostly Pushtun
   truckers.

2. A. Q. Khan, the Father of the Pakistani Nuclear Bomb, is
   an al-Qaeda sympathizer, and he and the other elite atomic
   scientists around him have had contacts in the past with Osama
   bin Laden and other al-Qaeda leaders. For years Khan ran
   a covert arms trade business, swapping bomb-making technology and materiel for missiles with North Korea and for

cash with Iran and other nuke-hungry nations. Through him, al-Qaeda has a direct conduit to some of the most advanced weapons systems in the world, and, almost as important, to the *sub rosa* transportation system that moves military contraband around the globe. The cigarette smugglers were funneling a percentage of their profit to the Shi'a group Hizbollah in Lebanon.

3. The South Asian Drug Mafia: Both Taleban and al-Qaeda are deeply involved in the South Asian heroin business, which brings in hundreds of millions of dollars in profits every year. Now that they have set their own network of heroin labs inside Afghanistan, in Helmand Province and other areas outside the control of the Kabul government, they keep much more of the money than they did when they supplied raw opium and morphine base to heroin manufacturers in Pakistan and Tajikistan. Most Afghan heroin goes to markets in Pakistan, Iran, and the former U.S.S.R., and al-Qaeda personnel; the connection north through Tajikistan gives al-Qaeda valuable ties with the Russian Mafia, which is a known conduit for weapons buying, illegal immigrant smuggling and the like. Afghan heroin makes it to Western Europe via the Turkish crime syndicate and the Albanian Mafia, which is deeply embedded in the governments of both Albania and Kosovo.

4. Snakeheads and Coyotes: Millions of illegal immigrants move across the world every year, transported by professional

smuggling rings like the Chinese "Snakeheads" and Mexican "Coyotes." A young Chinese man or woman in the hopeless rural backwaters of Fukien Province can pay a Snakehead agent a five or ten thousand thousand dollar down payment and end up in New York, Vancouver, or Los Angeles. Similar smuggling routes run from the Balkans and the former Soviet Union, and from al-Qaeda hotbeds like North Africa, Kurdistan, and Pakistan; many end up in Western Europe, but the destination of choice is the United States, usually by way of Mexico or Canada. There are now Mexican Coyote gangs who specialize in smuggling Arabs and other Middle Easterners from Mexico across the border into the U.S.; both the Shi'a extremist group Hizbollah and al-Qaeda have ties to these groups.

It is pathetically easy to run illegal immigrants across the Mexico-U.S. border, using the same techniques employed to bring drugs in. Criminal groups with their own paramilitaries control whole towns on the border, and have purchased large ranches near the frontier where their activities can't be controlled. Mexican locals have a saying about such ranches: "The turtles eat well there," meaning that trespassers end up dead and dumped in the river. In some cases, smuggling gangs have bought or leased ranches on the U.S. side of the border, giving them a safe transshipment point for marijuana, heroin, "dirty bomb" materiel, or a team of al-Qaeda operatives, whatever pays.

Who even has a clue if al-Qaeda has a headquarters, in the corporate sense of the word, or where or what it is if they do? An office building in Riyadh? A palace complex out in the Saudi desert (some are Disneyland-sized)? A compound in Rawalpindi? A warehouse on the outskirts of Houston?

Yes, its training camps in Afghanistan are gone, but according to writings posted on the Internet by al-Qaeda tacticians they had proved to be of little use anyway. The camps were mainly involved in training insurgents, large numbers of them, from all over the Moslem world; they were then supposed to return home and wage war on the pro-Western regimes there, but as one al-Qaeda leader pithily put it, "The trainees were eager to come and be trained as insurgents, but it turned out they were a lot less eager to go home and join an insurgency."

Abu Mus'ab al-Suri, the Syrian engineer who until his death in April 2006 was one of the most prescient and innovative jihadi strategists, urged Islamic terrorists to give up the idea of large boot camp–like military training facilitates and concentrate instead on forming small terrorist cells in safe houses and "small, secret mobile camps" inside the countries to be attacked. According to al-Suri, the fate of al-Qaeda and Taleban in Afghanistan demonstrated the dangers of training large numbers of recruits openly, in either friendly countries like Taleban-ruled Afghanistan or lawless territories such as Somalia. These non-covert activities inevitably bring retaliation from the enemies of the jihad; not only that, jihadis are vulnerable to being apprehended when they travel to the countries they are going to attack.

If nineteen young men armed with box cutters and stun guns can strike a near-mortal blow against the most powerful nation on earth, why bother to maintain a huge network of training camps along with the conventional military forces necessary to protect it? The 9/11 hijackers were recruited in Europe and the Middle East and indoctrinated in Afghanistan, and some were trained at flight schools in the United States, but they just as easily could have gone through the same process at a mosque in New Jersey, or a condominium in Aspen.

Despite al-Suri's fears about the dangers to terrorists on the move, there are repeated signs that members of this new kind of al-Qaeda are here, there, and everywhere today, traveling with impunity, and that we seem to be powerless to stop it. Like the iceberg that sank the Titanic, it's drifting somewhere out there in the fog and the dark of night, most of it underwater, invisible to our eyes; but it would be a fatal mistake to think that it isn't there, *somewhere.*

1. On July 11, 2005, four important al-Qaeda detainees escape from a high-security U.S. prison inside Bagram Air Base in Afghanistan. Mahmud al-Qahtani from Saudi Arabia, Abdullah al-Hashemi from Syria, Omar al-Faruq from Kuwait, and Abdullah Abu-Yahya al-Libbi from Libya turn up missing during an early morning check of the cell block; their orange prison coveralls are found later, concealed in a clump of bushes near the jail facility.

To anyone familiar with Bagram, the escape seems inexplicable. Simply finding your way around inside the enormous facility is almost impossible without a guide. The base perimeter is secured by mine-fields and razor wire, and is patrolled twenty-four hours a day. The entire area around the base is a special high security zone: for miles in every direction the roads are controlled by checkpoints manned by pro-American Northern Alliance guerrillas armed with AK-47s, RPG-7 grenade launchers, and heavy machine guns.

Immediately after learning of the escape, the U.S. military distributes hundreds of photos of the four men to Afghans living near the base; every vehicle entering or leaving the surrounding area is stopped and searched, and dozens of locals are detained and questioned, including at least one prominent Northern Alliance commander. The security crackdown is so draconian that Afghans who live in the area orga-nize a demonstration outside the base's main gate, protesting the mass searches and arrests. Despite it all, the escapees' trail is stone cold.

In the months following their escape, the four fugitives seem to be everywhere. Mahmud al-Qahtani turns up in the Khost area in southeastern Afghanistan, where Taliban and al-Qaeda forces are fighting a bloody campaign against U.S. troops and Afghan govern-ment authorities; then he is spotted in Iraq, where he carries out two highly publicized beheadings of prisoners held by al-Qaeda.

Al-Faruq, born in Kuwait to Iraqi parents, was al-Qaeda's chief of operations in Southeast Asia when he was arrested by Indonesian authorities in June 2002, before being turned over to the U.S. and ending up at Bagram. Now the Indonesian government fears he will return to their part of the world to carry out retaliatory strikes.

But Abdullah al-Libbi is by far the most dangerous of the four; a brilliant tactician and eloquent speaker, he frequently appears on al-Qaeda videotapes in the months following his escape. Many counter-terrorist experts regard him as a prime candidate to succeed bin Laden himself if the current terrorist leader is ever killed or captured.

2. Pakistani authorities announce they have trapped "a leading terrorist figure," perhaps Osama bin Laden himself, in a village in the tribal area of the North West Frontier Province, along the Afghanistan border. Pakistani troops surround the village, and after several days of fighting they succeed in occupying it, but the terrorist leader, who turns out to be one of the heads of the Uzbekistan arm of al-Qaeda, is gone: the Pakistanis say he escaped through a hitherto-undiscovered mile-long tunnel under the Afghan border.

3. Another "important al-Qaeda leader," a man reportedly involved in the group's program to develop weapons of mass destruction, is spotted in the mountainous Pankisi Gorge area of Georgia, an area frequented by pro-al-Qaeda Chechen terrorists. Georgian security forces aided by U.S. Special Forces troops mount an operation to capture him, but with no luck. Two or three weeks later the man is reported to be in the tribal

area of Pakistan's NWFP, having somehow crossed a half dozen borders and two thousand–plus miles of hostile territory undetected. After the reported sighting in the NWFP, he is never seen again.

4. U.S. intelligence officials announce a worldwide lookout for thirty-two-year-old Ms. Aafia Siddiqui, an "angelic-looking" Pakistani-born MIT graduate described by the FBI as having the ability for "planning and facilit[ating] . . . attack[s] against the United States." Siddiqui was last seen in Boston in 2003, and may now be in either Pakistan or the U.S., nobody knows; she reportedly has the ability to pass as either a native-born American or Hispanic, thanks to a long period of residency in Texas. She and her former husband, Harvard University–trained anesthesiologist Mohammed Amjad Khan, are reported to have purchased night vision gear, body armor, and military manuals during their time together in the United States. Like Siddiqui, Khan is considered a threat to plan, organize, and carry out terrorist attacks in the U.S., and like her his whereabouts are completely unknown; he could be anywhere, from Falls Church, Virginia, to the Khyber Pass to the Gulf Emirates.

5. Twenty-eight-year-old Adnan Shukrijumah, of mixed Saudi/ Caribbean heritage, is another terrorist suspect, whereabouts unknown, with a "chameleon-like" ability to change his appearance. A skilled commercial pilot and computer programmer, he possesses American, Canadian, Trinidadian, and Guyanese

passports, and is able to function easily in this country, thanks to fifteen years spent in Brooklyn and Florida. He has also lived in northern Mexico and Canada, and is a suspect in the theft of 180 pounds of radioactive material from a Canadian university. Suspected of helping plan future terrorist attacks inside this country, he remains at large despite a $5 million reward for his arrest.

6. Five years ago, dock workers at an East Cost port opened up an apparently empty shipping container, part of a cargo that had just arrived from overseas. They found the interior had been outfitted as a kind of second-class ship's cabin: a power source, lighting system, bedding, chemical toilet, ventilation, evidence of food storage and preparation, everything necessary to survive a lengthy voyage from, say, Aden to Newark, or Istanbul to Philadelphia. There was no sign of the one or more occupants and their luggage. (A Soviet RA-115 tactical nuclear device can fit into a large suitcase, and a single physically-fit individual could carry one for miles if necessary.)

7. In 2006, Border Patrol agents along the Arizona-Mexico border warn that illegal Mexican migrants who recently converted to Wahhabi Islam, the fundamentalist school of Islam that spawned al-Qaeda, Taleban, and other extremist/terrorist groups, have been crossing into the United States accompanied by Middle Eastern Wahhabi "missionaries" posing as Hispanics. A smuggling ring specializing in smuggling Middle

Easterners into the U.S., run by a former Mexican consular officer in Lebanon and the Arab-Mexican owner of a San Diego restaurant, is broken up. In two incidents in the same month, Border Patrol agents capture seventy-seven Arabs in the Chiricahua Mountains of Arizona, but report that many more members of the groups, maybe two hundred, escaped. When they are caught, Middle Eastern border crossers are never questioned, due to lack of interpreters; they are simply bused back across the border to try again, or, even better from their point of view, released on their own recognizance to appear at deportation hearings sometime in the future.

CHAPTER 8

OUR OWN WORST ENEMY

On January 20, 2007, five members of an elite U.S. Army Special Ops team were killed in Karbala, in southern Iraq. Initially the military reported that the soldiers, who were said to be on some kind of Civil Affairs mission for the 412th CA Battalion, were killed "by mortar and small arms fire" somewhere on the city's outskirts, but that story proved to be false. Gradually the true story came out. The five men, thirty-one-year-old Captain Brian S. Freeman, twenty-two-year-old Specialist Jonathan B. Chism twenty-five-year-old Private First Class Shawn P. Falter, twenty-five-year-old 1st Lieutenant Jacob N. Fritz, and twenty-year-old Private Jonathan Millican, were elite soldiers, on an important mission, briefing Iraqi authorities about Iranian Revolutionary Guard penetration of Shi'ite groups; they had with them a laptop computer containing highly classified intelligence on the subject. And they weren't killed in a meeting engagement or ambush in the city streets or out in the countryside, but in a surprise attack in the supposed safety of the central Iraqi government compound in Karbala, a fortified

installation housing a large number of Iraqi troops, whose only entry
point was a well-guarded gate.

The men who killed them were described as "looking American or
European," wearing American uniforms, led by a "blond man speaking perfect English"; they knew all the current passwords and security
protocols for getting past Iraqi police and military checkposts, including the guards at the gate. They entered the compound in two or
three black SUVs, bypassed all the buildings housing Iraqis, and went
straight to the offices where the American team was staying. Captain
Freeman was killed, and the other four soldiers taken prisoner, probably with the aid of stun grenades or "flash-bangs." Pausing to blow
up several vehicles parked in the compound, the terrorists escaped
with their captives and the computer they had come after. The four
soldiers were found later, shot execution-style, a hundred miles away.

Months later the U.S. military claimed they had tracked down
the minor Shi'ite leader who supposedly contracted out the operation, but reading between the lines it seems highly unlikely the real
perpetrators were ever identified or punished. Were they European
al-Qaeda "A" team members working on behalf of the radical al-Quds
Brigade of Iran's Revolutionary Guard? Even though al-Qaeda has
slaughtered Shi'as in Afghanistan and Iraq, and Iran is a Shi'a state
which arms and trains Iraqi Shi'as against al-Qaeda and other Sunni
groups, that scenario is far from impossible. The key operative phrase
in the East, cliché' though it may be, is still "The friend of my enemy
is my enemy; the enemy of my enemy is my friend." Or were they

Al Quds agents who learned their tradecraft from al-Qaeda? The point is, nobody really knows; and either way, the attackers were far more skilled in special operations, black ops, or whatever you want to call them, than their counterparts on our side. We pride ourselves on our high-tech eavesdropping, our commo intercepts and ability to process raw data into tactically useful intel, but the fact remains, the Bad Guys knew exactly who and where the Good Guys were, and how to get to them . . . and, of course, they got away with what they wanted, the computer that revealed who our intelligence sources inside Iraq's radical Shi'ite groups were, and how much they had told us. It seems almost certain that al-Qaeda or someone very much like them has somehow penetrated the most sensitive and closely guarded inner sanctums of our counterintelligence/counter/terrorist establishment.

In 2004, I spent six months with CAT-A 13, a seven-member U.S. Army Civil Affairs team working in Khadimiyah, a Shi'ite neighborhood on the left bank of the Tigris River. The team was part of the 425th CA Battalion (Reserve), based in Southern California; though like all CA troops they were underfunded and undertrained in key areas like spoken Arabic, the 425th accomplished remarkable things during their one year deployment in Baghdad. (That is a whole other story: how we are neglecting the very institutions, like Civil Affairs, AID, and the Peace Corps in the all-important fields of nation-building and winning hearts and minds, and instead entrusting the bulk of the job to longtime Pentagon contractors who are both incompetent and corrupt. Several books could be written on the shameful role of the private sector in sabotaging our efforts in Afghanistan and Iraq, and you would have to build a hundred Guantanamos to house the guilty parties.)

I lived and worked 24/7 with CAT-A 13 in order to write a book on how Civil Affairs teams operate, but much of what I saw and heard there didn't fit into the resulting book, *Waging Peace: A Special Operations Team's Battle to Rebuild Iraq*, which was about the proud history of CA and the accomplishments of a single seven- person CA team in one Shi'a neighborhood in Baghdad. Other material, including my close-up view of the American counterintelligence/counterterrorist effort in Iraq, was not part of the story. What follows are just a few notes on the subject.

When I was in Iraq, most of the violent resistance to the U.S. occupation still came from homegrown Sunni and Shi'a groups like the clan-based guerrillas in Anbar Province and the foot soldiers of the radical young Shi'a cleric Muqtada al-Sadr. At the same time, al-Qaeda suicide and car bombers were attacking Shi'a targets explicitly to trigger a Sunni-Shi'a civil war. In fact, the night before I joined the team in Khadimiyah—my first few weeks in-country I had been going out with other elements of the 425th, including the medical/public health contingent and the team attempting to rebuild the Abu Ghraib neighborhood—al-Qaeda members attacked the al-Khadimiyah Mosque, the third most important Shi'a shrine in the world, just two blocks outside the main gate of Banzai FOB (Forward Operating Base), where CAT-A 13 was based. The measured response to the subsequent Shi'a riots by the 1/5 Cav, the combat arms unit responsible for security in Khadimiyah, was a key factor in CAT-A 13's successful CA mission in the neighborhood. Colonel Miles Miyamasu, the brilliant, tough CO of the battalion, ordered his men not to fire on the mob unless they were clearly and unmistakably in mortal danger. Humvees were battered and SAW-gunners were hit with stones, but not a single shot was fired in retaliation. The Shi'a clerics from the shrine who virtually ruled the central core of Khadimiyah couldn't help but compare the Americans' response to what Saddam and company would have done. Indeed, there was a whole government warehouse in Khadimiyah full of chlorine gas canisters, enough to kill every man, woman, and child in west Baghdad; former Ba'ath regime officials claimed it was for "water purification," but the canisters bore Iraqi Air Force markings, and along with the chlorine were the necessary chemicals to weaponize the gas. Compared to Saddam, the infidel soldiers from America looked pretty good. Thanks to this initial event and the continued work of the Cav and the CA team from the 425th, Khadimiyah was one of the few bright spots in 2004 Baghdad in terms of security, local government, civic action, and quality of life.

Unfortunately, places like Khadimiyah were comparatively rare. In Iraq as a whole we were way, way behind the eight ball, to the point of near-stupefaction. The lack of contact and communication between American civilians and soldiers and Iraqis was surreal. The first two months I was in Iraq, one of our Iraqi interpreters repeatedly told us that Uday Hussein's chief bodyguard, still a heavyweight figure in the

Ba'athist resistance, had infiltrated the Green Zone in the guise of a taxi driver, using his access to identify important Iraqis working for the U.S. and ID them for elimination. For eight weeks the interp, who moonlighted working undercover for U.S. Army intelligence, warned everyone he could think of, including his intel bosses, but no one cared enough to listen and take action. Finally, he alerted some Gurkha security guards he knew, who passed the info up the line, and the Green Zone authorities issued a warrant for the bodyguard's arrest. Someone must have been working undercover for the Bad Guys, though, because the next day the bodyguard and his taxi never showed up; in fact, the man was never seen again. In another case, this same interpreter penetrated one of the insurgent groups who regularly mortared and rocketed the Green Zone; the gang was rounded up, only to be realeased three weeks later due to influential Iraqi friends in the Coalition hierarchy. The problem was, no one on the American side had any idea of who the good and bad Iraqis were; our impressions were filtered through the language and cultural barriers, and the suffocating layers of security that sealed the decision-makers in the Green Zone off from the reality of life outside the wire, in Iraq. (Rajiv Chandrasekaran's book *Imperial Life in the Emerald City* is the quintessential source on the subject; it reads like *Catch-22* meets *The Quiet American*.)

In another case, high-ranking American officers and Coalition civilians discovered an Iraqi painter who did world-class portraiture, incredibly lifelike, for one tenth of what they would have cost back in the U.S. The portraits seemed like perfect souvenirs of one's deployment in Iraq, and they became a kind of fad among the movers and shakers in the Green Zone: soon everybody who was anybody had been painted by the Iraqi portraitist or was in the process of arranging a sitting . . . that is, until American soldiers raided an insurgent safe house in Baghdad and discovered photographs of all the portraits, tagged with names, official titles, travel habits, and so on: a group wanted poster of all the key officials in the Green Zone, to help speed their demise.

Probably the biggest ongoing security breach in Iraq involved the Arabic language interpreters attached to every military unit and civilian office. Unbelievably, Donald Rumsfeld, General Tommy Franks, and company did nothing to increase the number of available Arabic speakers in the months leading up to the invasion of Iraq. It was such a low priority that when a significant number of the top Arabic students at the army's Monterey language school turned out to be homosexuals, they were summarily expelled from the program.

When American troops rolled into Iraq, they quickly discovered that they couldn't communicate with the Iraqi people. There is a very funny video on YouTube shot recently by soldiers in Iraq: their Humvee has pulled over a carload of suspicious-looking Iraqi men, and one of the GIs yells at the occupants in a perfect Southern sheriff voice: "Get—out—of—the—ve-hi-cle." No reaction. Louder: "GET—OUT—OF—THE—VE-HI-CLE." No response. Still louder and angrier: "GET—OUT—OF—THE—VE-HI-CLE!"

And then the punch line: "GET OUT OF THE VE-HI-CLE, OR I'LL TEACH YOU HOW TO SPEAK ENGLISH!"

Among the makeshift attempts to break the language barrier were fold-out sheets with cartoony images of everything from various weapon types, kinds of military encounters, injuries to different areas of the body, kinds of poisonous snakes and insects, etc., so that the GI in the field could simply hold the page in front of an Iraqi, point to the appropriate picture, and pantomime ignorance. Later, I heard of a portable squawk box, to be carried on convoys and patrols, with prerecorded Iraqi phrases on the order of "Get the @#$*& away from my Humvee," "Drop your weapon, NOW!" and, no doubt, "GET OUT OF THE VE-HI-CLE!" Not exactly ideal "hearts and minds"-winning material.

Of course, the results of the lack of communication was anything but funny. The bloodshed in the Sunni Triangle, which claimed the lives of hundreds of Americans and thousands of Iraqi civilians, began when the 82nd Airborne first occupied Fallujah and set up their command post in a local school. That night, a crowd of parents gathered, shouting demands that the U.S. troops move to a different building so their children could return to school the next day. To the Airborne troops, a bunch of Arabs yelling "Give us back our school!" sounded like "Kill the infidel Crusaders!" The troops panicked and opened fire, killing and wounding dozens and triggering an escalating cycle of violence that eventually resulted in the virtual destruction of the entire city, home to nearly half a million people.

Exacerbating all of this was the *laissez faire* subculture of the intelligence community in Iraq. I never knowingly met any CIA personnel, but the FBI and Army intel I encountered were a dubious bunch. The medical team of the 425th was housed at Baghdad International Airport, next to the FBI agents' residence; the agents were there on six month tours, basically to punch their career tickets, and none of them I talked to had any knowledge of or interest in Iraq, Islam, or anything else related to their job. One thing they did like was a good party. Our battalion medic was roused late one night to help revive a newly arrived agent who had overdosed on alchohol and tranquilizers, and another agent had to be disciplined for crudely propositioning female soldiers after drinking too much at one of the hellacious fetes at the FBI house.

Mililtary intel types were more varied; some were extremely smart and hard-working, studying Iraqi Arabic in their few non-working hours, sharp people, and others were like their FBI cousins, seeming to be marking time before returning stateside. You often heard the latter boast about how drunk they were going to get when they got home, and complain about how much they loathed Iraq, often within earshot of their Iraqi field agents. Once, in the Green Zone, I happened upon a going-away party for a young Army MI type; his Iraqi colleagues had brought a whole banquet of local delicacies, kabobs, roast chickens, rice, fish, that their wives had stayed up all night preparing. After a few minutes of nobbling at the food, the party's honoree suddenly announced that he and his American buddies were leaving for another, better party, "where there may be some booze," and they walked out, leaving the Iraqis standing there with all that beautiful, lovingly prepared food. They looked at each other and at me with those woebegone expressions Iraqis seem to excel at. I thought that a couple of them were actually going to burst into tears. It was one of those excruciating moments that make one wish they could instantly dematerialize.

One thing you learn in the Moslem world is that manners can actually save your life; I am not exaggerating, and I'm not the only person who has experienced this firsthand. My good friend, Swedish Johnny, an ex-Marine sniper who worked for Blackwater in the Shi'a Triangle in Iraq, had a gift for getting along with the locals: he was actually interested in their culture and religion, liked the country, and formed genuine friendships with unlikely types like Shi'a imams and men who confessed they moonlighted as anti-U.S. guerrillas. One time his Iraqi friends took him aside and told him, "Don't ever stand next to that man there," indicating another Blackwater employee who was loudly disdainful of Iraq and everything in it. When Johnny asked why, they told him, "Because we've decided to kill him. He insults our people, our faith, and our country. We hate him, so he is going to die. We don't want you to get hurt when it happens."

Another time, when he was up north in Mosul, Johnny encountered an American soldier who made a point of going out every morning, standing on top of a vehicle, and urinating in plain view of the Iraqis passing outside the wire. There had been no violence at this outpost, no shooting, bombing, or rioting, for months. One morning just like any other, the man clambered up onto his perch, unzipped his pants, and a moment later his skull literally exploded as a high-powered round from a Dragonov sniper's rifle struck him smack in the middle of his forehead.

If the locals don't like you, you may or may not get killed, but you definitely won't get good intel out of them; which is exactly what sabotaged our war against al-Qaeda in Mesopotamia.

When I was in Iraq in 2004, Abu Musab al-Zarqawi was just making a name for himself there, beheading prisoners on camera, attacking Shi'ite religious processions, blowing up Shi'a mosques and shrines: his avowed purpose was to trigger an ethnic civil war in Iraq, sabotaging our plans for the country to become a beacon of peace, tolerance, and security. At the same time he was making the gap between Iraqis and Americans even wider: soldiers began to view all locals as potential kidnappers and executioners, journalists stopped going out and talking with Iraqi civilians, and civilian aid workers fled the country. And, just as important, he continued to distract the United States from what should have been our primary concern, Afghanistan and Pakistan, the real focus of al-Qaeda's global strategy.

Now, al-Zarqawi never became a popular figure in Iraq: he was a foreigner, a Jordanian, a petty criminal and ex-convict, unprepossessing in appearance, and below average in intelligence. So you

would think, with all of our resources, we would have been able to
kill or capture him in short order. Instead, he operated successfully
for over two years, until June 2006, when he was finally killed in
an air strike. And, this is very important, *we didn't track him down
through human intelligence; we ran him to ground through an elaborate
mix of homing devices, electronic eavesdropping, and aerial surveillance.*

Why didn't the Iraqi people turn him in? Because we had so few
people in-country who could even talk to them, let alone bond with
them, let alone get them to like us enough to help take down someone who, by all accounts, they were hardly fond of in the first place.
A bad show, to say the least.

And we didn't kill him until he had carried out his mission: by
destroying the golden dome of Al-Askaria Mosque, one of the holiest
half dozen sites of Shi'a Islam, early in 2006, he caused the final break
between Sunni and Shi'a Iraqis; that attack and the Shi'as' retaliation
that followed marked the end of the myth of a new, ethnically unified
post-Saddam Iraqi nation, a myth that has still not revived, despite
the continuing presence of 120,000 plus American troops.

That is what is called a Catastrophic Intelligence Failure; especially in a war like the present one, in which force and firepower are
trumped time and time again by knowledge.

And our failings transcend intelligence; they permeate the entire
struggle over the hearts and minds of the world's Moslems.

On May 31, 2006, a U.S. military convoy from Bagram Air Base,
speeding into the crowded streets at the northern edge of Kabul,

slammed into an intersection crowded with vehicles and pedestrians. Approximately a half dozen Afghans were killed and scores more injured. When some in the crowd threw rocks at the American vehicles, someone reportedly panicked and opened fire with a light machine gun as the convoy left the scene at high speed. As word of the incident spread through the city, mobs of tens of thousands of rioters swept through the streets, attacking, looting, and burning aid offices, NGO and UN vehicles, businesses, Western residences, and hotels. For an entire day the whole city was a scene of total anarchy as police abandoned their posts and foreigners hid away in their compounds. It was as if everything the United States and its foreign and Afghan allies had accomplished in the capital since taking over from the Taleban in the winter of 2001 was swept away in twelve hours.

I had been in Kabul soon after Taleban was ousted, and reading about the riots back in the States I remembered how boundlessly hopeful things had seemed then. Allied convoys driving through the city had been cheerd by crowds of pedestrians; a lone Westerner like me could walk alone at night without any qualms. On Chicken Street, all the old tourist shops were open, and off-duty American GIs joked and bargained with shopkeepers and passersby.

What had happened? A lot of it had to do with the slow pace of reconstruction and recovery, and the corruption that ran rampant in every sector of life. Just one example: the traffic police in Kabul were notorious for shaking down motorists and extorting bribes, and taking advantage of the opportunities hundreds of fake policemen had appeared; dressed in ersatz uniforms of varying quality— one Afghan friend told me you could always spot the phonies because they wore battered sandals instead of boots, and another told me he had been accosted by one and prepared to baksheesh him until he noticed the man had drawn an array of medals and ribbons on his shirt in ballpoint pen!—they lurked wherever the real cops were absent, doing the same business of flagging down drivers and taking their money to release them. As the legitimate police were really no better than than the copycats, it was hard to tell them apart. Just how extreme the lawlessness in Kabul had become was drama-tized by what happened when the government announced a plan to crack down on the *faux* police: the counterfeit cops announced that they would paralyze the city in retaliation by stopping virtually every driver they saw, and literally thousands of them appeared en masse, demonstrating for their right to take part in the systemic looting of the public. Their point was simple: if everyone else was doing it, including the "real" police, why couldn't they?

When corruption becomes the subject of endless joking it is usu-ally way past the point when it is really funny; but there was another reason for the rage in the city, one that the U.S. could have, should have easily avoided. A few months before the riots, a friend for-warded me an e-mail from an American officer stationed at Bagram, about the increasingly bad behavior of many U.S. troops and the sub-sequent deterioration of American-Afghan relations. It seems that some particularly unenlightened sergeant-major types had showed up in-country determined to "show them Afghans who's boss around here." They instituted news ROEs, Rules of Engagement, for U.S. convoys and vehicles: for "security's sake" they would no longer obey local Afghan traffic laws, but would drive at high speed, run civilians off the road, keep nonmilitary vehicles away at gunpoint, and, if they encountered any injured Afghan police or soldiers, even if they themselves were the cause, they would not stop to give medical assistance. According to the e-mailer, within days the whole mood of Kabul changed: treated like enemies or inferiors by the American military, formerly friendly locals began calling them "the new Russians," and stories, some highly exaggerated of course, began to multiply, of insults, accidents, and provocations by GIs. Compounding all this were the contractors from DynCorp and other contractors who sped through the city streets late at night, drunk, shouting and honking their horns. The writer predicted that all this would have extreme consequences; tragically, he was proven right.

I returned to Kabul a few months after the riots, and the friendly, open-hearted city I had seen last time was gone. There were no more GIs shopping on Chicken Street or anywhere else; foreign pedestrians were virtually non-existent. When I went out with my Afghan friends to late-night restaurants, locals stared at me like I was a man from Mars. Every Afghan I know had a horror story, usually several, about my countrymen: being deliberately run off the road on the way to school, cursed and threatened by SAW-gunner on a Humvee, the whole gamut of rudeness. "Who's running this show?" I asked myself. "Or rather, who isn't?"

I have had the pleasure of spending time, lots of it, with U.S. Army and Air Force Civil Affairs teams in Iraq and Afghanistan, soldiers whose behavior was a constant credit to our country and which constantly won respect and affection from the locals; and I have been around combat arms units, like the 1/5 Cav, who are similar. But the mindset of some other troops—and the attitude seemed to spread from the top down all too often—was so bad it virtually sabotaged the very mission they had been sent to carry out. They were sent to provide security for nation-building efforts and to help create allies; they ended up creating enemies and undermining the reconstruction process. One war correspondent friend of mine summed it up this way, talking about a certain ill-mannered army division that seemed to be running an al-Qaeda recruitment campaign wherever they were deployed: "These guys are like your drunken brother-in-law; you don't want to take him out in public anywhere, because he always causes trouble and ruins everything for everybody."

CHAPTER 9

THE NEXT 9/11

He was fat, urbane, and affable-looking, clad in a hip designer jeans and two-hundred-dollar basketball shoes, an iPod dangling on his chest. We were both sitting in the international transit lounge at Dubai airport, waiting patiently for flights to Europe. He told me he was a sometime student from Brunei, the immensely rich petro-sultanate in the Indonesian Archipelago, on his way to London for an open-ended holiday. I told him I had been working in Iraq, helping with reconstruction, which drew an approving nod and smile. Then I told him I had been working in a Shi'a neighborhood in Baghdad; his smile didn't change, but he made a mild clucking sound of disapproval and said, "Oh, we think that Shi'as aren't really Moslems; they're really heathens."

"But that's terrible!" I responded. "With all the enemies Moslems have around the world, you people should stay united."

"That will never happen," he laughed. "We have a saying: 'Moslems will stop killing Moslems the day the world ends.'"

Hate is the power that drives al-Qaeda, the Moslem Brotherhood, the Deobandis, Taleban, the Wahhabis, and all the other Salafi off-shoots in the world; hatred, frustration, and humiliation. Even if we managed to eliminate al-Qaeda, more such groups would inevitably appear, like the heads on a hydra.

The problem is, there are reasons for the hatred, real reasons. Thomas Hardy's great poem "The Convergence of the Twain" inspired by the Titanic's sinking, traces the births and the trajectories of existence of the two looming entities, one the very paradigm of joy, purpose, "progress," and human life itself (and ultimately folly, too, Hardy implies), the other the cold, faceless, all-destroying juggernaut of nature that ultimately grinds up and devours even our greatest, proudest creations. The two are inexorably fated, Hardy says, to come together in the end, and when they do the *Titanic*, like the *Pequod* in *Moby Dick*, is doomed: all ships are ships of fools, just as all empires delude themselves that they are eternal, even as the barbarians are scaling the walls. Hardy's final lines could easily have been written in 2002:

> Till the Spinner of the Years,
> Said "Now!" And each one hears,
> And consummation comes, and jars two hemispheres.

Al-Qaeda and Salafism are human creations, of course, unlike icebergs, but the forces behind them transcend reason and rationality: they are cloaked in theological terms, but they have to do with the most basic human needs, emotional as well as physical.

Declaring war on these forces is kind of like retaliating for the *Titanic's* sinking by bombarding the Arctic ice pack; all you do is create more icebergs.

What we are facing is a sociocultural "Perfect Storm": a vast array of countries with failing economies, moribund political systems, and soaring populations; in which upward mobility is stifled by corruption and ever-decreasing opportunity; in which vast numbers of under-employed young men are tantalized with images of material success, glamour, and sex by the global media, and simultaneously frustrated, enraged, and humiliated by the lack of all the above in their everyday lives, and the apparent impotence of their faith in Chechnya, Palestine, Kashmir, Burma, and a dozen other lands, drummed into their consciousness 365 days of the year by al-Jazeera, al-Arabiyah, the popular tabloid press, and the fiery sermons of mullahs, imams, and sheikhs.

"Western-style democracy" does not address any of these very real grievances; in fact, it requires a certain level of prosperity, social contentment, and secular tolerance to even survive, let alone flourish. You could say it is a symptom of a successful society, not the means to one. And it is a fragile institution: the last true democractic election in Algeria put into power a fundamentalist Moslem coalition that would have sooner rather than later outlawed the very democracy it rode to power, and no one doubts the same thing would happen if Egypt ever became a democracy. Pakistan began life as an explicitly secular democracy, but ethnic strife and pandemic corruption exacerbated by rampant overpopulation has produced a kleptocracy with increasingly mafia-like political parties overseen by a bloated military. (None of this is exclusively a phenomenon of Moslem countries, by the way: democracy thrives in Moslem Indonesia and Turkey, died in Buddhist Burma, and is on increasingly shaky ground in Hindu-dominated India.)

Salafism, promulgated and funded by Saudi Arabia, offers a simple, attractive way out for a certain percentage of the population of these dysfunctional societies. Salafi congregations re-create an imagined, paradisical past in the present: by emulating the simple, austere lives of the original Moslems, they reimagine a world in which Islam was an unstoppable force, conquering everything in its path, spreading righteousness throughout the world. But this of course is not enough: the corrupt, unjust reality around them must also change; and, as that reality and all it partakes of is beyond redemption, worse than nothing, if everything and everyone needs to be destroyed along with it, so be it. To the Salafis enemies are everywhere, as they aggressively attempt to convert the *ummah*, the community of 1.1 billion believers around the globe, all Moslems who disagree with them are *kfirs*, outsiders and enemies. Christians and Jews are deluded and beyond God's salvation,[6] and all the rest of humanity,

---

[6] Sadly, there is little to choose between the three great monotheistic faiths when it comes to tolerance. When I was in Iraq, the U.S. soldiers were on average conspicuously less tolerant than Iraqis we met. Many of the Shi'as wanted to discuss the similarities and differences between Islam and Christianity with

idolaters, materialists, atheists, and polytheists like Hindus and Buddhists are even worse. Further, in one of his self-described *fatwas*, bin Laden proclaimed a doctrine of permissible collateral damage similar to the one espoused by the United States in its unlovelier moments: even if it takes the lives of innocent Moslems, an attack or operation aimed at Islam's enemies is blameless, as long as real damage is inflicted on the enemy. He was referring to the embassy bombings in East Africa, which killed many local Moslems.

The Saudi Arabian government has built and funded hundreds if not thousands of Wahhabi mosques and *madrassas*, from Indonesia to Thailand, Pakistan to the Balkans, Holland to the United States, that teach Wahhabism's pathological creed. Like Christianity and Judaism, the teachings of Islam contain a wealth of self-contradictory, wildly divergent assertions, ranging from the tolerant and big-hearted to the bigoted and vindictive. Wahhabi teachings cherry-pick the Koran and the Hadith, the body of sayings and incidents credited to the Prophet, for the nastiest, most unenlightened passages. The Prophet's attitude toward Jews and Christians, for instance: at one point, good Moslems are urged, in effect commanded, to pay respects to a Christian's or Jew's funeral procession just as they would a Moslem's. Wahhabi schools in Saudi Arabia and elsewhere avoid any mention of such ecumenical

---

Americans, but were almost always rebuffed with statements like, "My God isn't like your God—mine is the only real one."

attitudes, mentioning only examples from the opposite side of the ideological spectrum, like this quote attributed to Mohammed himself, from a textbook for fourteen-year-old boys:

> The day of judgement will not arrive until Muslims fight Jews, and Muslims will kill Jews until the Jew hides behind a tree or stone. Then the tree or stone will say, 'Oh Muslims, oh Servant of God, there is a Jew behind me. Come and kill him.

Other Saudi texts teach that Shi'a Islam is a "Jewish plot" against the true Islam; that Moslems should never be friends with Christians and other non-Moslems, or assoociate with them at all, in case they are cajoled or tricked into less-than-hostile feelings; and that Wahhabi Moslems will eventually convert the entire human race by rhetoric or the sword, and kill anyone too incorrigible to "choose" "salvation."

During the last half of the twentieth century, Salafi anti-Semitism took on a markedly European flavor, de-emphasizing religious differences in favor of physical caricatures and crude physiognomic stereotypes in its cartoons and poster art; ironic, in that Arabs, of course, are at least as Semitic as their Jewish counterparts, and the same swarthy, big-nosed faces mocked by racist propagandists in Riyadh and Rawalpindi could be used just as well to mock the petro-sheikhs of Arabia. Much of the blame for this mingling of different flavors of hatred can probably be traced to the little-known role of Joseph Goebbels, the Nazi Party's propaganda wizard, in assisting the Egyptian Moslem Brotherhood in attracting new supporters. Goebbels paid for a new, modern printing press for the Brotherhood, and provided them with Arabic translations of European anti-Semitic "classics" like the *Protocols of the Elders of Zion*. This influence persists today: the *Protocols* (they are a forgery, originally produced by Czarist Russia's secret police to "prove" the existence of a centuries-old Jewish conspiracy against Christian Europe) still show up regularly on bookstore shelves from Pakistan to Londonistan. (Which brings to mind a sad little historical footnote. I have a Pakistani film director friend, descended from a long line of artists, mystics, and literati from Lahore, Afghanistan, and as far afield as Uzbekistan's Ferghana Valley. Back in the 1930s, one of my friend's uncles, a writer, traveled to Europe, became involved with Max Reinhardt's theater group, and married a young German Jewish actress. When the Nazis took over, both of them vanished into the inferno of the death camps. My friend's uncle, dark, with typical Afghan/Central Asian lineaments, was as inevitable a casualty of the Third Reich as his wife.)

The lack of logic implicit in Salafism's racist propaganda takes nothing away from its power to inflame the masses in the streets of Cairo and Karachi, the impoverished *fellahin* of the Upper Nile and Sind, the alienated second and third generation immigrant kids in England's Midlands, Paris's *bidonvilles* and anomic public housing projects, the Africans displaced by imperialist diamond and coltan wars selling smuggled cigarettes and cloned cell phones on the sidewalks of Rome and Barcelona, the latter-day Qutbs scowling and whispering in the campus coffee lounges of second-rate universities. Not only don't we have a PR machine in place to counter radical anti-Westernism—when the State Department tried to kickstart an international advertising campaign to boost the image of the United States in the Islamic world and elsewhere, one wit came up with "America: More Than Fat People with Bombs"—we lack a credible message to deliver.

*   *   *

They seek him here, they seek him there:
Those Frenchies seek him everywhere.
Is he in heaven or in hell
That damned elusive Pimpernel?

—Leslie Howard in the title role
of *The Scarlet Pimpernel*, 1934

The town of Zhob lies between South Waziristan and Wana, in the tribal area of the North West Frontier Province of Pakistan. It was originally called Fort Sandeman, and some maps still display both names, Zhob first and the other below, in parantheses. Robert Sandeman was one of the greatest of the British Political Agents who helped rule the Empire's frontiers during the nineteenth century, using a canny blend of armed force, bribery, and divide-and-conquer diplomacy to try and prevent outright anarchy among the tribes that straddle the Afghan-Pakistan border. These tribal people have never been conquered, even by conquerors and empire-builders like

Alexander the Great, Suleiman the Magnificent, and Babur. Even today, the government of Pakistan has little or no control over most of the tribal area, and Taleban and al-Qaeda operate there openly.

Backtrack from Zhob a ways, toward the troubled territory of Waziristan, and then make a sharp left turn, to the Afghan border; cross a razorback ridge, and there, in the middle of absolutely nowhere, a valley winds northwest into Afghanistan. The only egress to the valley is from its mouth; the country on either side is surreally rugged, a heaving chaos of barren hills sliced by mazes of dry riverbeds, *nullahs wadis*; an army could get lost in there forever, and never be found.

You find people almost everywhere you go in Afghanistan, in the most inhospitable of places, but not here, not in these hills. For hundreds of square miles, there is nothing but an abandoned compound here and there, mud walls melting into the earth like pale chocolate, and the ghost of what might have once been a road, a trail, a long, long time ago . . .

The landscape inevitably makes you think of poetry, T. S. Eliot's "The Wasteland," to be specific:

Here is no water but only rock
Rock and no water and the sandy road
The road winding above among the mountains
. . .
There is not even silence in the mountains
But dry sterile thunder without rain
There is not even solitude in the mountains

But red sullen faces sneer and snarl
From doors of mudracked houses

And here is a mystery: what is a well-graded, all-weather road doing, entering the valley at the Pakistan border and following the valley bottom for mile after mile, with side roads and trails leading off everywhere? Why is there a guard post at the frontier, and what looks like a whole elaborate system of other checkpoints? What are these trucks carrying, that travel between the valley and Pakistan constantly?

There are no smuggling routes here: this part of the border is over a hundred miles from the nearest major poppy fields, and even further from Chaman and the Khyber Pass, where weapons, commercial goods, and God knows what else cross the frontier from Afghanistan into Pakistan regularly. Which brings up something else about this road: insead of continuing on to Ghazni or Gardez to link up with the interior of Afghanistan, it dead-ends in the valley, in the heart of those desolate hills. The nearest Afghan towns are many miles from the end of the road, far beyond the head of the valley, across more trackless, intractable hills. Whatever is going on in this valley, it has to do with Pakistan, and the greater world beyond . . . perhaps as far away as the grand throne rooms of power, on the banks of the Potomac and the Hudson . . .

The road through the valley is strange enough, but even stranger, more incongruous, are the buildings and other man-made features

scattered along its length. Not Eliot this time: the poetic lines that
come to mind now are by Wallace Stevens, writing about a glass jar
placed on the floor of a wild hardwood forest:

> It did not give of bird or bush,
> Like nothing else in Tennessee.

Indeed: like nothing else in this empty corner of Afghanistan.
There is so much inexplicable development going on in the valley
that one doesn't know where to begin. The large octagonal mosque,
roofless, never quite finished, with its rows of marble columns. The
skinny T-shaped structure overlooking what looks like a parade
ground. The little clusters of cottages, each, interestingly enough,
out of line of sight from the others, and each with a neat little patch
of lawn out front (*lawns*, in rural Afghanistan?). Buildings that
look an awful lot like weapons bunkers, right down to the earthen
berms surrounding them. In shadowy side canyons and at the base
of cliffs, warrens of what look like tunnel entrances, reminiscent of
the famous Taleban/al-Qaeda bases at Tora Bora and Zawar Khili;
some of those subterranean passageways extended thousands of
feet through the mountains, with rooms that could hold a thousand men. (Are those vent outlets, covered by concrete cones? What
is *under* the valley, anyway? Was it Scheuer who said that it's all
going on beneath the surface? Out of sight, out of mind, as the
saying goes?)

Notably absent on the surface are the mud-walled compounds you would expect to find in the eastern Afghanistan countryside. And also notable, given the number of buildings in the valley and the volume of traffic on the road to Pakistan, is the lack of anything resembling a village center or bazaar: no shops or stalls strung along the road, no *chaikhannas*, or caravanserais with trucks and buses laagered inside walled yards. Whatever this valley is about, it isn't traditional farming, or commerce, or any other licit activity you would expect in this neck of the woods . . .

But if not that, then what?

And what are they plotting and planning, in their hidden redoubt, wherever that might be?

From past deeds and words, another major attack or set of attacks on the order of 9/11 would be characterized by the following:

Simultaneity: Attacks on different targets at the same time. We know that bin Laden wants al-Qaeda to be viewed as a major player, on the same level as leading nation-states, and that means the ability to project one's power over long distances and in different places at the same time. Such attacks could overwhelm our overtaxed resources to the breaking point. What if there were chemical attacks causing hundreds or thousands of casualties targeting Camp Victory and the Green Zone in Baghdad Bagram Air Base and the U.S. Embassy in Kabul, and at the same time here in the U.S the Holland and Chesapeake Bay Tunnels and the New York subways, Washington's Metro system, and San Francisco's

BART were hit with conventional explosives, killing hundreds and trapping hundreds more underground?

Theatricality: Al-Qaeda is extremely media-conscious and savvy; bin Laden realizes that if a building falls in a city and no one anywhere else sees it fall, live on television, in a very real sense it hasn't happened at all. Imagine a *Die Hard* sequel, but one in which the Bruce Willis role is filled by Michael Chertoff, backed up by the FEMA bureaucrats of the New Orleans hurricane debacle. Rush hour in San Francisco, a rainy, fog-shrouded evening: two semis drive onto the Golden Gate Bridge simultaneously, one from each direction. At the same moment they swerve left fom the righthand lane, smashing cars, jamming the bridge with wreckage as they come to a stop. As the drivers jump down from their cabs and walk away, explosions crumple the trucks' trailers, dumping tons of thermite and other chemical incendiaries onto the pavement and simultaneously releasing clouds of chlorine, mustard gas, and CS. Within minutes motorists trapped on the bridge are leaping off into the cold waters far below to escape the gas. Emergency crews rush to the scene, to try and contain the thermite before it eats through the structural supports of the bridge, but every time they start working conventional explosives triggered by timers drive them back with heavy casualties. News helicopters capture the chaos.

Scale: A chemical weapon attack on the New York subways three years ago was reportedly called off by al-Zawahiri at the last moment because the estimated death toll, approximately three thousand, was deemed insufficient. There are definite indications that the al-Qaeda leaders want their next attack to be much, much larger, in terms of economic damage and numbers of dead, than 9/11.

Weapons of Mass Destruction vs. "Found Weaponry": There is plenty of evidence that bin Laden and company would *like* to employ WMDs, nuclear, chemical, or biological, against the West; the problem is, that is easier said than done. Despite the weaponized anthrax accident that killed seven hundred or more of civilians in the Sverdlovsk area of the Soviet Union in the pre-*glasnost* era, that kind of death toll is not easily achieved; the huge casualties in the Sverdlovsk incident would have been greatly reduced if authorities had not attempted to cover up the nature of the disaster, hamstringing the response of an already-substandard public health system. Similarly, attempts by al-Qaeda affiliated groups in Iraq to couple chlorine gas with conventional IEDs and VIEDs have proved barely successful. And the oft-bruited "dirty bomb," which spreads radioactive material via conventional explosions, is not an automatic recipe for success, either: to spread enough material over a wide enough area in a form that makes decontamination difficult and time-consuming is extremely challenging.

What many find disturbing are the repeated promises of future "Hiroshimas" in American and European cities by al-Qaeda leaders, and the repeated rumors of stolen Soviet RA-145 tactical "suitcase" nukes being bought and sold, along with the fact that no big-time buyers of nuclear material or devices have ever been apprehended in places like Moldavia, where purloined Soviet military property most frequently goes up for sale on the Black Market. A number of small-time amateurish retailers and would-be buyers have been caught, often in Sting-type operations, but the sellers are cheap-suited petty hoods selling bogus products like so-called "red mercury," or negligible amounts of potential weapons materiel, hardly enough to fuel a good sneeze, while the purchasers are just middlemen hoping to resell some place down the food chain; no Russian Mafia bosses in diamond necklaces flogging latchkey nukes to sheikhs in Gulfstreams.

The reason I think is obvious: big-time professional fences and smugglers and their customers remain in business because they are very, very good at what they do, which means that they know how to do business discretely, and because the enormous profits they earn buy a correspondingly enormous degree of security. Smuggling of antiquities, drugs, "sex slaves," counterfeit luxury goods, and illegal immigrants is now virtually institutionalized, nearly immune to detection and interdiction, even on the American side of the U.S.-Mexico border. When I was researching the narcotics business in Southeast Asia, the U.S., and elsewhere years ago, I got to know a mid-level Columbian cocaine wholesaler in the San Francisco area; I asked him once about the risks in bringing the stuff into the States, and he laughed: "You think we stand on the beach at night with a flashlight, hoping the Coast Guard doesn't show up while we unload some old boat? It's not like that. It comes in on a schedule, like once every two weeks or a month, and everyone is paid off; it's like we're bringing in lettuce from Sonora or beef steaks from Argentina. Then it's stored in warehouses and sold off when the market is most favorable. If you read about some stupid *cabrone* with a spare tire full of blow getting busted trying to drive across at El Paso, or a Convair 580 with two tons on board that loses an engine and lands on Interstate 10 outside of Phoenix at rush hour, *it's not one of us, or anyone we know. We're the ones no one ever sees or hears about.*"

There is no reason to think that the WMD business is any different. In fact, an economist looking at the consequences of the breakup of the Soviet Union, the quick profits made by those who looted the old infrastructure and sold it off, the extreme poverty of most of the rest of the society (including its former watchdogs) together with the limitless financial resources of wealthy Saudis, would probably say that such trafficking is inevitable, in this era of free trade and fallen borders. In the breakaway Rhode Island–sized Transdneister Moldavian Republic, over 70 percent of the economy is based on the extralegal sales of locally manufactured weapons, including Stinger-like shoulder-fired missiles and lightweight Alazan weather research rockets jerry-rigged with radioactive "dirty bomb" warheads; thirty-eight or more of the latter are known to have disappeared into the global marketplace, and some have already been used against civilian targets in interethnic conflicts in the Caucasus. Other Moldavian-made weapons have showed up as far away as West Africa. Moldavia is so desperately poor that a black market gang was arrested there last year for cutting up human corpses and selling the flesh as "pork" in the public marketplaces; the only major exports besides arms are the country's young women, who are sold as chattel sex workers to mafias in the Balkans, Israel, and western Europe.

There is also no reason al-Qaeda could not have acquired its own nuclear arsenal through official channels, without skulking around Tiraspol, the shabby capital of the Transdneister, or on the back-road contraband routes through the Carpathian Mountains. It is a well-known fact, as noted before, that A. Q. Khan, founder of Pakistan's nuclear weapons program, is an admirer and sometime associate of Osama bin Laden, and that many in his coterie of assistants and acolytes share his jihadist sympathies. And why assume that Vladimir Putin would try to block the transfer of Soviet WMDs to al-Qaeda? Putin is no friend of the United States, and his regime is already a prime suspect in the radioactive poisoning of at least one prominent anti-Kremlin Russian émigré in the United Kingdom. As long as the transfer can be blamed on "theft" or "corruption," it's really a no-lose situation for Mr. Putin, and as a longtime KGB professional he would have no trouble engineering such a covert operation.

At the same time, the 9/11 attacks themselves showed how WMDs and other high-tech weapons are not the only way to topple an empire.

The series of enormous truck bomb attacks on Kurdish Zoroastrian villages last year very well have been rehearsals for similar attacks here in the U.S.: the explosions were so huge that each bomb virtually gutted an entire village, causing hundreds of deaths and hundreds more severe injuries. Imagine the effects of a similar blast trapped by the tall buildings of Wall Street in New York, or Washington D.C.'s K Street, also known as Lobbyists' Row.

Or what if ten or a dozen suicide bombers struck crowded polling stations up and down the East Coat on Election Day? Wouldn't the elections be suspended for security reasons immediately? And how many Americans would suspect the Bush Administration of being in on the attacks? What would that do to the already shaky institution of democracy in America? There were definitely signs that al-Qaeda was preparing to sabotage the last presidential election, in 2004: rumors of strike teams moving into position south of the border, chatter on the Internet about midget submarines and remotely piloted seafloor exploration vehicles in Boston Harbor (close to the Democratic Convention site), credible stories of corps of suicide bombers being readied in Wahhabi mosques across America. For one reason or another, nobody pulled the trigger: very possibly because the plans were not perfected to bin Laden and al-Zawahiri's satisfaction—al-Qaeda would rather hold off for a few years to eliminate any chance of failure than strike earlier and risk a humiliating setback that would compromise its leadership of the global Salafi/jihadi movement.[7] But a presidential Election Day, with its

---

[7] One thing to really worry about is the competitive nature of the international Salafi/jihadi community. Al-Qaeda is just one of several groups competing for the same recruits, money, power, and prestige: this is probably one reason we haven't

supersaturated live media coverage around the globe, would present al-Qaeda with the ultimate in McLuhanesque soundstages, the greatest scene-stealing opportunity in history.

Speaking of suicide bombing, the stealth weapons system of al-Qaeda and Taleban ...

Much nonsense has been written in this country about Islam as a culture of death and Moslems as "natural" suicide bombers. Suicide fighters are as old as the most archaic forms of tribal warfare; Plains Indians who belonged to special fighting corps known as Contraries or Brave Hearts used to tie themselves to stakes driven into the ground and cover their fellow-warriors' retreat, fighting on with bows and arrows or guns until they were finally killed, or charge on horseback headlong into the enemy ranks. They were greatly feared because of their utter fearlessness.[8]

During the Second World War, Shinto kamikaze units in explosives-laden planes and suicidal manned torpedos, and banzai-charging infantrymen, played a large part in Japan's defensive strategy as the borders of the Greater East-Asia Co-Prosperity Sphere shrank ever closer to the Japanese home islands: the hope was that America could be literally bled into a truce short of outright surrender. Japan

---

seen another mega-attack since 9/11—the catastrophic consequences even a partial failure would bring. Ironically, it also helps guarantee another, bigger 9/11: al-Qaeda's continued pre-eminence in the movement depends on their eventually striking a major blow against the American homeland again.

[8] "You love life, so you are afraid to lose it. We Moslems love death, so we are never afraid." —al-Qaeda video

may have been deficient in manpower, firepower, hardware, and resources, but they could prevail by being stronger in spirit.

The modern era of suicide bombing began on May 21, 1991, in the south Indian village of Sriperumbudur, when a female member of the Sri Lankan seperatist group the Tamil Tigers approached Indian Prime Minister Rajiv Gandhi with a wreath of flowers, knelt before him, and detonated an explosive-filled vest, killing herself and him. Suicide bombing quickly became a favorite weapon of the Tigers in their war of secession against Sri Lanka's Buddhist majority. Only later did it become popular among Palestinians and in the Chechnyan war against Russia.

When I was in Iraq in 2004, Sunni groups were using it successfully against U.S. and Allied occupation troops and Shi'a civilian targets, mostly the latter. The great majority of the bombers, both vest-wearing individuals and drivers of vehicular bombs, were non-Iraqis; at least half were Saudi Arabians and citizens of other Gulf emirates. Interestingly, in Saudi Arabia, a tightly controlled police state with virtually no civil liberties, radical mullahs had no problem recruiting bombers from among the kingdom's masses of underemployed young men, training them in mosques and *madrassas*, and sending them across the border into Iraq, sometimes via a third nation like Syria, where they were cached in safe houses and base camps before being equipped with a lethal vest or vehicle, assigned a target, and being sent into action. At one point, there was reportedly a backlog of scores of trained bombers waiting in the pipeline to be deployed.

Volunteers were showing up from near and far. When fingerprints were taken from the severed hand of one successful car bomber, he turned out to be a Lebanese who had been turned away by immigration authorities while trying to fly into the U.S. two or three years before. Another bombing was carried out by a young Belgian woman recently converted to Islam.

A few months ago, Pakistani Taleban leader Baitullah Mehsud released a video of the graduation ceremony for two hundred students at a school for suicide bombers in South Waziristan. The ceremony was held in an open field, in broad daylight; the faces of the graduates were cloaked, so they couldn't be identified. When Mehsud spoke of future suicide bombing targets, he included London and New York, along with hints that bombers might be carrying more than plastic explosives and ball bearings; something much, much bigger, in fact.

I don't know if any of the Waziristan trainees were bound for the United States; there is no real reason they couldn't be, given the ease of entering Mexico, the wide-open human trafficking pipeline across the border into this country, and the fact that hundreds of Middle Easterners have been among its successful customers. At the same time, it would be perfectly easy to train and equip bombers right here, in the many Wahhabi mosques and *madrassas* the Saudis have built on American soil.

One I know of is a fortess-like edifice in Falls Church, Virginia, near the Seven Corners shopping center, less than ten miles from the U.S. Capitol. The mosque's mullah is on the board of at least one ecumenical interfaith board espousing cooperation and tolerance between Christians, Jews, and Moslems; strange for a leader of a faith that thinks of its fellow-monotheists as kin to apes and pigs, perhaps, but useful if one wanted to establish one's quid pro quos as a nonthreatening, beyond-suspicion hale-fellow-well-met kind of Wahhabi.

They are practically everywhere. When I was last in Gallup, New Mexico, at the eastern edge of the Navajo Indian Reservation, the most visible large-scale construction project I saw was that of the town's new Wahhabi mosque, within sight of Interstate 40. According to people in law enforcement, Wahhabi *madrassas* can teach their students how to make a suicide bombers' vest, how to conceal it, and how to use it, without breaking the law; they can't be arrested until they actually tell their students to put their vests on, go out into a public place, and blow themselves up.

Al-Qaeda has been actively seeking Western members for several years now, Americans, Canadians, or citizens of the EU of European ethnicity; recruitment efforts in Bosnia, where many Moslems have brown or blond hair and fair complexions, and adapt easily to living in the West undetected, no doubt have a similar motive. Some Albanian Moslems look like Mullah Omar, but most resemble Tony Romo, George Clooney, or Amy Winehouse. I often wonder whatever became of all those American Black Muslims who visited Jalaluddin Haqqani back in the 1980s and

'90s: some were rumored to be army or marine veterans, and they were so passionately anti-American/European that more than once they had to be restrained from beating visiting foreign journalists to death . . .

I can see clearly in my mind's eye a Hindu Kush version of that Cold War–era KGB training center in which recruits were taught to speak, act, dress, and think like Americans before being lofted like human ICBMs toward the continental United States. Imagine a string of walled compounds, each out of sight from the other, in a remote canyon—sometimes the students sit outside on the lawn for lectures and hands-on training—and each a separate "college," specializing in a different target country. Adam Yahiye Gadahn ("Adam the American"), the ex-California hippie and outspoken prophet of his homeland's doom ("If you convert now, you won't automatically go to Hell when we kill you; and if I were you, I would convert now rather than later!") would be an important figure there, dean of the faculty as it were, greeting new students as they arrived by truck, blindfolded or hooded, from the nearest Pakistani military air strip (built with some of the billions of dollars paid annually to Pakistan to fight Taleban and al-Qaeda).

The students would never even necessarily know what country they were in, though some of them could probably make an educated guess. Nearly seven years have passed since 9/11: plenty of time to graduate hundreds of people, men and women, and broadcast them like dragons' teeth around the world.

The point is, the next wave of attackers won't be "young males of Middle Eastern origin"; they may just as well be a Swedish women's ski club on holiday, or a party of "Japanese businessmen" (Malayan or Sinkiang Chinese checking out real estate in Miami, casino sites in Vegas, or opportunities for upscale condominium projects in L.A.'s Koreatown . . . not worth a second glance.

But back to suicide attacks: historically, they are a weapon of last resort for rebels, insurrectionists, maquis, partisans; the poor, the outgunned, the occupied, the vanquished or dispossessed. They are called "terrorists," in part because empires don't employ suicide fighters (because they don't need them), and partly because empires are the ones that write the rule books and decree what is right and what is wrong. Scouring an entire valley of all human life with carpet-bombing B-52s, defoliants, and antipersonnel mines sewn piecemeal from eight miles high is not terrorism, basically, because *empires, one's own at any rate, don't commit terrorist acts.* This is morality on the order of "He who has the gold makes the rules," or the Red Queen's "It's so because I say it is," and, alas, we are no more innocent of it than Genghis Khan or Suleiman the Magnificent.

To many in the unaligned nations of the world, suicide bombing doesn't look that different morally from bombing from the air; it all depends on the target, the motive, the degree of provocation. What if the French Resistance had employed suicide tactics against the German occupation? The black South Africans against the

Dutch Afrikaners, in the wake of the Sharpeville Massacre? When an American pilot deliberately flew his crippled, burning plane into the funnel of a Japanese ship during World War Two rather than parachuting, deploying his life raft, and hoping to somehow survive, the same American newspapers that excoriated the "fanatical Japs" for their kamikazes and banzai charges extolled his "All-American courage" and "red-blooded guts."

Moral equivalence aside, suicide bombing has turned out to be the Salafis' ultimate offensive tool, impossible to stop and available in endless numbers. In Afghanistan, it has proven to be an insoluble problem, derailing reconstruction and nation-building and making normal life almost impossible.

The suicide bombers killing American soldiers in Afghanistan today are being recruited and trained by ISI officers in the border areas of Pakistan. Most captured terrorists tell the same story: how they were recruited by offers of money, appeals to religious fervor, or, often, by threats of retaliation against their families if they refused; how they were trained and armed in camps run by the Pakistani Army; and how before they left Pakistan they were told what targets to attack inside Afghanistan, often by Wahhabi mullahs from the Saudi-financed fundamentalist *madrassas* that have sprung up all over Pakistan in recent decades.

Others have turned out to be alcoholics or drug addicts, young men disgraced in the eyes of their family and society; they are offered a one-time chance for salvation by their cold-bloodedly priestly mentors. (The Palestinian/Israeli film *Paradise Now* portrays the whole sordid process of cynical manipulation brilliantly.)

You may laugh, but the sexual nature of the rewards promised to martyrs in the hereafter are a powerful motivating force for uneducated young men in societies where opportunities for normal male-female relationships before marriage are nil. Go into the lobby of a cheap hotel in Peshawar and observe the crowd of Pakistani youths, all dressed up with no place to go, clustered around a television that is inevitably tuned in to Indian MTV; they stand there for hours, not saying a word, their eyes fixed on the shimmying Nautch dancers from Bollywood movies and musical acts like the Supermodels, whose sensuality is magnified a hundredfold by the arid womanless atmosphere of a city where a single veiled woman shopper is a rarity.

And now of course the suicide bomber phenomenon has spread back to Pakistan, in another classic instance of "blowback," an intelligence operation that rebounds on its creators. Suicide bombers have already made normal life in Afghanistan almost impossible; now it threatens to do the same in Pakistan.

People who live in target-rich highly mobile environments, people like us, are the perfect suicide bombing target, of course. When Homeland Security puts out one of their heightened threat level assessments, it is difficult not to burst out laughing; the fact of the matter is, the threat we are facing can take so many possible forms that it is impossible to protect against even a fraction of them.

Consider this: since 9/11 scarcely a month has gone by without a terrorist attack or the threat of one, but it is almost certain that none of them was planned and funded by Osama bin Laden and the core leadership of al-Qaeda. They were the work of local al-Qaeda-inspired organizations, small ad hoc groups, or individuals. Even al-Zarqawi, the late founder of Al-Qaeda in Mesopotamia, organized the group on his own, and during its first months of existence he and his followers were repeatedly criticized and all but ostracized by al-Qaeda's central command; in their scheme of global strategizing, it was far too early to be going on the offensive in what was the heartland of the old caliphate. Countless messages from al-Zarqawi complaining of lack of aid and begging for more support were intercepted during that period. It really wasn't until bin Laden recognized the nuisance value of al-Zarqawi's destructive activities in Iraq—and the value of Iraq as a recruiting tool, insurgent training area, test site for new weapons, and continuing diversion of American attention and resources from Afghanistan and Pakistan—that al-Qaeda grudgingly allowed al-Zarqawi into the fold.

In bullfighting there is a word, *espontáneo*, describing spectators so inflamed by the action in the arena that they leap from the stands and join in. The same thing is going on all across the Islamic world, and though these unskilled amateurs usually fail in their efforts by talking too much about them in advance or bungling some technical aspect of the operation—the faulty bombs that didn't explode in what was to be phase two of the London public transport attacks are a good example—they are sometimes spectacularly successful. The crash of EgyptAir Flight 990 on October 31, 1999, is almost certainly an example. The New York–Cairo bound Boeing 767 crashed at 1:50 a.m., a short time after taking off from JFK; among the 217 passengers on board were 34 high-ranking Egyptian military officers, twenty of whom had just finished training as Apache helicopter pilots; they were slated to join Egypt's antiterrorist counterinsurgency forces upon their return home. All of the officers had boarded the plane in California. From analyzing the plane's black box and the cockpit voice recordings it seems almost certain that one member of the flight crew, who had been behaving strangely during the crew's stay in a New York hotel, deliberately put the plane into a dive and then shut down the engines; one or more of the other crew members fought to regain control of the craft but failed; and the plane ended its 33,000 foot dive by smashing to pieces in the sea off of Long Island.

Given the target-rich nature of the industrialized world, its extreme vulnerability, and the availability of endless information on methods of mass destruction on the Internet, even a single angry jihadi could inflict serious damage on the New World Order. For instance, a matchbox full of lethal rubber tree parasites, transported from Amazonia, where the trees are immune, to Southeast Asia, where they are not, could wipe out most of the world's natural rubber production. Car tires would not be affected—they are made

from synthetic rubber—but the big tires on modern jets depend on natural rubber's unique resistance to heat and friction. This would not mean the end of life as we know it, but the synchronicity between, say, a half dozen such attacks could have the impact of another Pearl Harbor.

CHAPTER 10

HOW TO LOSE/WIN A WAR IN THREE EASY STAGES

Ever since 9/11 we have been painstakingly, doggedly writing the book on how to lose a war: first, by mistakenly calling it a war; second, by mistaking who the enemy is, and where the battlefield; and third, by having no idea why we are fighting, what victory would mean, and how to get there from here.

In contrast, the other side has a divinely ordained sense of purpose, and, just as important, *they believe they are winning*, I am not the only observer who felt extremely uncomfortable about the series of video and audio proclamations issued by al-Qaeda leaders a year and a half ago. It wasn't what they said half as much as the way they said it: their air was unmistakeably smug, supercilious, like someone dictating surrender terms to a defeated enemy, or a poker player about to lay a royal flush on the table with all the chips in the world in the pot. Their general message was, *We've warned you time and time again to change your ways, but you just wouldn't listen; well, sorry, but now it's too late.*

When you factor in al-Qaeda's 2003 plans to gas the New York subways with cyanide-dispersing devices (referred to as *mubtakkar* in Arabic), plans that were supposedly forty-five days from fruition when canceled, it is hard not to take al-Qaeda's apparent confidence at face value; as mentioned earlier, Ayman al-Zawahiri reportedly called off the operation because the projected death toll, three thousand, was not big enough, and there have been hints that al-Zawahiri and company were waiting for much bigger weapons, nuclear devices to be precise, to be smuggled into the U.S. Since then, there have been repeated references to "American Hiroshimas" and the destruction of entire cities like Washington and New York by a variety of al-Qaeda and al-Qaeda-linked leaders, from Iraqi Kurdistan to the Tribal Area of Pakistan.

Remember, jihadism is a highly competitive business, and if al-Qaeda produces too many empty threats with no follow-up actions for too long they will eventually begin to lose their cherished position as the industry's undisputed leaders.[9] This primacy is obviously vitally important to bin Laden and al-Zawahiri, who view themselves as the legitimate theological and strategic leaders of the global jihad.

---

[9] Which makes al-Qaeda's failure to claim credit for either the Madrid train bombings or the assassination of Benazir Bhutto sinister indeed. A group that didn't have much bigger plans in motion, plans which they were certain would be successful, would have leapt to claim at least a partial role in such spectacular and media-dominating operations.

While it's probably true that al-Qaeda can't actually win their war—it's difficult to imagine a planet-wide Salafist caliphate emerging in the twenty-first century—it is certainly true that we can lose it. In fact, we probably are in the process of doing just that, not because of al-Qaeda's actions but because our reactions to them. Bin Laden is definitely aware of this, and the whole context of asymetrical warfare: he has publicly boasted about how fifteen young Moslem men with box cutters and a few tens of thousands of dollars behind them caused tens of billions worth of damage to the American Empire. If anything, he drastically understated his case. Today, seven years after 9/11, we see an America that has retrogressed to the mindset of nineteenth-century gunboat diplomacy, mistaking "boots on the ground" and far-flung military bases for signs of real power abroad ("The sun never sets on the Pax Americana"), while our educational system, physical infrastructure, balance of trade, environment, and quality of life at home deteriorate to ever-lower levels of quality.

An instructive little anecdote: a government Iran-watcher I know was screening Iranian government news programming the other day, and happened upon footage of a laboratory in Teheran where serious-looking young women in traditional *chadors* were doing stem cell research—research approved by the country's Shi'a religious leaders and praised for its benefits to mankind, in contrast to the limitations put on such research in the United States of America, once the undisputed scientific and technological capital of the world.

• • •

People who surrender their liberty for the sake of security deserve, and get, neither.

—Benjamin Franklin [revised]

And the truth of the matter is, we are less secure than ever; al-Qaeda is still out there, and our futile attempts to fight it have only multiplied the numbers of our potential enemies in the Moslem world; in countries like Jordan and Egypt, where 60 percent or more of the population once viewed the United States favorably, we are now regarded as the worst nation on earth by more than 80 percent of the people.

Something is very, very wrong.

When we drove the Taleban out of Afghanistan, 95 percent of the Afghan people loved us.

When we overthrew Saddam's regime in Iraq, two-thirds of the Iraqi people were grateful.

Today, a majority of the people in both countries want us gone. Afghans are starting to call U.S. soldiers "the New Russians." Most Iraqis now think we invaded their country to steal their oil, not to liberate them.

It would be a mistake to blame the changes completely on our enemies. The truth is, in both countries we have been "ugly occupiers." Almost all the American civilians who have gone to work in Iraq and Afghanistan have no interest in the local people and no affection for them; they are motivated by greed. Many American soldiers sincerely try to help the Iraqis and Afghans, but they have been given almost no training in the locals' customs, language, or way of life. And as both countries have become more violent, and there are fewer and fewer opportunities for soldiers to get to know the locals, and vice versa, too many soldiers now view the locals, as enemies instead of allies; not surprisingly, this becomes a self-fulfilling prophecy, as soldiers react recklessly to every perceived threat, killing innocents, and high ranking officers lose sight of their original mission and use air power against insurgents, with predictably destructive results toward "winning hearts and minds." Commanders in both Iraq and Afghanistan have done much to correct these errors on their own, but we need to back them up with dramatic increases in manpower and intelligence and Civil Affairs, not to mention honest civilian contractors motivated by patriotism, not profits, who actually care about the future of the countries they are working in, not to mention their own.

By the way, I don't blame any of the above on our soldiers in the field; never have American GIs been so badly prepared, poorly led, and given such confusing, paradoxical missions. And Rumsfeld and friends all but killed the motivating ideal of the citizen soldier by hiring their cronies' highly paid mercenaries to do for money what GIs have done for 260 years out of patriotism and the desire to help build a better world. It is close to a miracle that they have performed as well as they have.

Meanwhile, as far as our enemies are concerned, acquiescence emboldens evil, and the tragifarce of unpunished betrayal continues today. When I was in Iraq in 2004, nine tenths of the suicide bombers plaguing the country were from Saudi Arabia, yet military spokesmen, taking their cues from the neocons in Washington, always talked of Iranian and Syrian interference in Iraq, never mentioning the much greater role played by our Saudi "allies." Recently, the government in Baghdad estimated that at least 60 percent of the foreign terrorists operating in Iraq were Saudis, but the drumbeat of war talk aimed at Iran and Syria never completely dies down.

In Afghanistan, most of the bombers and insurgents come from training camps in the area around Quetta, in western Pakistan, where top Taleban leaders live openly in ISI villas, and from Waziristan, southeast of the Khyber Pass, which the government of Pakistan publicly handed over to Taleban and al-Qaeda groups last year. U.S. military officers in Afghanistan as well as Afghan prime minister Hamid Karzai and officials of his government in Kabul regularly condemn the tide of killers freely flowing across the border from Pakistan, but somehow it goes on unhindered. Scarcely if ever are they backed up by civilian higher-ups in Washington. In contrast, top administration officials reacted with a storm of outrage when weapons manufactured in Iran turned up in Taleban territory in southern Afghanistan in the last few years. Though the cache turned out to consist of just a few mortars, mortar rounds, and a small quantity of C4 explosives, you would have thought that Iran, not Pakistan, was the number-one villain in Afghanistan today. American officers on the scene were quick to point out that the provenance, even the real ownership, of the arms was far from certain: anyone, including Pakistan's ISI, could have purchased the materiel on the open market and sent it across the border into Afghanistan; not only that, the weaponry may not have been Taleban's at all, but supplies for the drug-smuggling mafias who control much of the region. Despite all this, Washington never backed off from its outraged chorus of "J'accuse, j'accuse!" It was a spectacle both surreal and obscene, when our real enemies were killing U.S. soldiers in both Afghanistan and Iraq. It hit me particularly hard: Sergeant Bob Paul, a member of the seven-member CA team I was with in Baghdad in '04, a brilliant, brave, funny, "always got your back" man, a true brother, was killed by a Pakistani-trained suicide car bomber in Kabul in 2007, and at the very least he is owed the truth.

So what do we do, beyond not fighting the wrong people with the wrong kinds of weapons, and driving away those who should be our allies?

We need to develop, with the urgency of the Manhattan Project and the sense of dedication and purpose of the Marshall Plan, a combination of the Peace Corps, Special Forces, Civil Affairs, AID, the old British Colonial Office, and Indian Civil Service. There are only four factors holding us back:

- We lack the necessary institutions.
- We lack the skilled, committed people to staff those institutions.
- We lack the educational system to produce those people.

- And we seem to lack the national will, the character, to create that kind of educational system.

We need ten, twenty times more knowledgeable, dedicated people living and working in Moslem lands, as teachers, paramedics, agronomists, engineers, and ten, twenty times as many young Moslems going to school over here.

We need to recognize our own role in creating Moslems who hate us, and develop new foreign policies accordingly, playing a more just and even-handed role in the Palestinian-Israeli conflict, and ceasing to automatically condemn every Islamic nation that sympathizes with the Palestinian cause as a "state sponsor of terrorism" and threaten it with forcible regime change.

We need to reach out to these comparatively moderate Moslems; in Afghanistan, we need to pour in the resources and security forces necessary to turn the country into a shining example of a strong, progressive Islamic state. All of this, I predict, would dry up nine-tenths of the pool of potential terrorists eager to attack us, leaving only those who hate us on purely irrational terms.

As for those remaining, those who recruit, pay, and send the suicide bombers and terrorists, the Salafist money-men and behind-the-scenes-masterminds—well, a GI friend of mine put it in these terms: "The only good Wahhabi is a dead Wahhabi." You can't coexist with someone who thinks Christians and Jews are descended from pigs and apes (and that Christians, Jews, Buddhists, Hindus, and Shi'a Moslems should be wiped from the face of the earth) any more than you can with a Nazi. We should make war on them until they are destroyed, but not with tanks and B-1 bombers: we need to use intelligence, paramilitary forces, black ops, assassination, sabotage, along with a huge dose of winning hearts and minds—the whole gamut of unconventional warfare.

"When you fight an insurgency, a bullet is more effective than a bomb," as the old saying goes. Any heavy lifting should be done by the great majority of non-Salafi Moslems who have been the Salafis' number-one victims, just as it was in Afghanistan, when Taleban and al-Qaeda were routed.

And we should do it while Washington and New York are still standing; and before the walls we are building around our country smother the very life out of us.